THE
DURGIN·PARK
COOKBOOK

THE DURGIN-PARK COOKBOOK

CLASSIC YANKEE COOKING IN THE SHADOW OF FANEUIL HALL

JANE & MICHAEL STERN

RUTLEDGE HILL PRESS™

Nashville, Tennessee

A DIVISION OF THOMAS NELSON, INC.
www.ThomasNelson.com

Copyright © 2002 by Jane & Michael Stern

All rights reserved. No portion of this book may be reproduced, stored in a retrieval system, or transmitted in any form or by any means—electronic, mechanical, photocopy, recording, or any other—except for brief quotation in printed reviews, without the prior permission of the publisher.

Published by Rutledge Hill Press, a Division of Thomas Nelson, Inc., P.O. Box 141000, Nashville, Tennessee, 37214.

Library of Congress Cataloging-in-Publication Data

Stern, Jane.
    The Durgin-Park cookbook / Jane & Michael Stern.
      p. cm.
    ISBN 1-40160-028-X
    1. Cookery, American—New England style. 2. Durgin-Park (Restaurant)
I. Stern, Michael, 1946- II. Title.
TX715.2.N48 S745 2002
641.5974--dc21   2002011873

Printed in the United States of America

03 04 05 06—5 4 3 2

Dedicated to

BERNICE & DAVID SCHERB

CONTENTS

FOREWORD

The Durgin Way

Since 1972, when our family picked up the torch from Jim Hallett, owner for over fifty years, we have carried the tradition started in 1826: simple Yankee fare made with the finest ingredients, prepared fresh daily in our kitchens. These characteristics have maintained the restaurant's landmark status around the globe. Our motto Your Grandfather and Perhaps Your Great-Grandfather Dined with Us Too, speaks to the loyalty of our customers across many generations. That loyalty is the result of a commitment of the owners and staff, the quality of the product, and the welcoming atmosphere of the restaurant. We appreciate our customers who dine at the restaurant time and time again. They are the men and women who know the staff by name and the menu by heart. Repeatedly, they have expressed gratitude that the décor and menu have remained unchanged over the years. Their loyalty contributes to the fabric of this very special restaurant.

The following stories, recipes, and photos will show you some of the men and women who have helped to make Durgin-Park the success that it is. Much of our reputation can be attributed to these people for the hard work, dedication, and personality that they bring to our restaurant. The casual, no-frills atmosphere, the family-style seating, the action in the kitchen, and the general hustle and bustle of the place make it a special place to be. We are proud of the fact that we have remained a unique restaurant. We celebrate this individuality and look forward to serving many generations to come.

As native Bostonians we welcome our patrons from lands near and far to experience our traditions, keeping in mind another Durgin-Park motto: There Is No Place Like This Place So This Must Be The Place.

—The Kelley & Solimando Families

ACKNOWLEDGMENTS

SEANA KELLEY and Suzanne Kelley, as well as chef Tommy Ryan, have helped us see beyond the institution that is Durgin-Park to the personality of the restaurant that they so expertly nurture and maintain. We thank them for their hospitality in Boston, as well as for sharing with us their stories, their expertise, and their enthusiasm.

Whenever we go anywhere to eat, we take with us our virtual companions at www.roadfood.com—Steve Rushmore Sr. and Stephen Rushmore, Cindy Keuchle, and Marc Bruno—good dining partners whose enthusiasm for Roadfood never flags.

Our own passion for Roadfood has been immeasurably enhanced by having this opportunity to create a series of cookbooks from America's most beloved restaurants, with Durgin-Park as our worthy emissary of classic Yankee cooking. Larry Stone, Geoff Stone, Bryan Curtis, and Roger Waynick are ever-present reminders that this book came into being because Durgin-Park is so deserving of it. Their passion makes publishing feel like a labor of love.

As always, it is with pleasure that we thank agent Doe Coover for her tireless work on our behalf, as well as Jean Wagner, Mary Ann Rudolph, and Ned Schankman for making it possible for us to travel in confidence that all's well at home.

INTRODUCTION

IF BOSTON IS the cradle of the republic, Durgin-Park is its commissary. The restaurant that indisputably boasts "Established Before You Were Born" came into existence a few decades before the Boston Tea Party as a place where the men who sold meat and produce in the city's Faneuil Hall Market could have a place to sit down and have their morning meal. Since the Civil War, just three families have owned it. The current chef, Tommy Ryan, has run the kitchen for more than forty years; before him, Edward "Babe" Hallett was chef for half a century. At Durgin-Park, tradition reigns.

Not everything about it is vintage. Sandwiches were added to the lunch menu in 2001, and pasta appeared a few years earlier for Boston Marathoners who needed to carbo-load. But the reason most people come to Durgin-Park is to have a time-honored, true-Yankee meal. When you sit down at a red-checked tablecloth in this boisterous eating hall, you fork into plates of such sturdy old-time delights as potted beef with onions, hand-patted fish cakes, broiled schrod, and oyster stew. Your meal starts with blocks of hot corn bread and creamy chowder; you can accompany immense slabs of prime rib with some of the planet's most delicious mashed potatoes; and you can top it all off with apple pandowdy or strawberry shortcake on a baking powder biscuit.

Durgin-Park sets the standard for Yankee cookery. Its stone-crock Boston baked beans and Indian pudding are definitive; the balance of its broad menu—Atlantic seafood and mighty cuts of beef—is timeless. And yet, for all its classicism, this is one of the most eccentric restaurants you will ever experience. Even its shape is unique and antiquated—a vertical space four stories above street level. The dining area is situated high above the sidewalk up a long flight of stairs. Cooked entrées are elevatored down via dumbwaiter from the third-floor kitchen to the waiters' station in the second-floor dining room. And if you think getting hundreds of hot plates from the third to the second floor during the busy supper hour is tricky, you should see the ancient rope-and-pulley system that is used to hoist great tubs of groceries up from the street into the upstairs kitchen early each morning. (On the floor above the kitchen is the house laundry and above that, the restaurant's offices.)

Before you eat at Durgin-Park, chances are good you will have to wait in line at the bottom of the stairs; and when space becomes available, you can look forward to a seat at a long table, elbow-to-elbow with strangers. Expect your waitress *not* to courteously introduce herself by name or to kindly inquire as to your well-being this fine day. Brusque service is part of the Durgin-Park package, and while today's wait-staff no longer offers what a headline writer once called "service with a sneer," neither do any of the veterans go out of their way to pretend that making and serving these heavy plates of food is anything but hard work.

In the kitchen you see just how much effort goes into Durgin-Park's menu. Everything is made from scratch right here, every day, most of it the very old-fashioned way. Dissatisfied with how the automatic peeler leaves flecks of skin on potatoes, Tommy Ryan has members of the staff inspect each spud and remove any imperfections before they are mashed. Likewise, carrots are peeled by hand with the same sort of little metal grater you might have at home. The son of a butcher who used to work in Faneuil Hall, Tommy is one of the few chefs who still buys "swinging beef"—large sections of cow to which he applies band saw and knife to cut steaks and chops just the way he knows they're supposed to be. Each fish cake this kitchen serves—and it serves plenty, especially on the side of Boston baked beans—is hand-fashioned; corned beef is corned on-premises; apples are peeled one by one in an old hand-cranked gadget, then made into applesauce; and gravy for turkey dinner comes from a roux that is whisked constantly until thick and mahogany brown.

"There is nobody in this kitchen who learned to cook in food school," Tommy Ryan says. "I have people who have been with me for fifteen or twenty years. They're the best because they came here knowing nothing and they learned how to do things the Durgin-Park way. I've had trained chefs, 'experts,' come in straight out of school, and they can't handle it. The pace and volume are too much for them. After a day, they run out in tears, crying, 'You're crazy!' Well, maybe we are, but it works. And it's worked pretty good now for a couple of centuries."

YANKEE CUISINE

AMERICA IS A land of myriad cuisines, many that come from around the world and some that have roots stretching back a millennium to the Native Americans who lived here long before European settlers arrived. What we now think of as traditional New England cookery certainly is newer than that of the Anasazi, whose likings have flavored the Southwest, but in some ways New England is the primary source of what we think of as basic American food. Ever since the Pilgrims learned about corn from the natives they met, Yankee cooks have set standards that, for better and for worse, have defined this nation's palate. It was in New England that our nation's first cookbooks were written and printed. Early in the twentieth century, *The Boston*

The pot pie is another Yankee square meal.

Setting the standard doesn't mean fancy. Meat and potatoes makes much of Yankee cuisine.

Although they will never enjoy twenty minutes of fame, Boston baked beans are always famous at Durgin-Park.

Cooking-School Cookbook made Fannie Farmer a national teacher, and that mantle was assumed later by another Bostonian, Julia Child (who originally taught us to master the art of French cooking).

For all its significance and influence, Yankee cuisine has remained resolutely untrendy. Other tastes and preferences regularly pop into our consciousness on the front page of the food section in newspapers—Cajun, Tex-Mex, Cal-Mex, New Southern, Old Southern, etc., etc.—while the cooking of the Northeast remains relatively stable, well-known but seldom celebrated.

One reason for its distinct lack of chic is that with rare exception and until only recently, New England cooking has always been primarily home cooking. Before Jasper White and Lydia Shire and Carol Peck, this part of the country had virtually no celebrity chefs to speak about, little ambition to be considered a fount of haute cuisine, and no show-offy dishes, such as blackened redfish or fajitas, that would make a big splash on the cooking segment of a TV show. The truly important New England

restaurants have never been deluxe, with kitchens that aspire to creative greatness; they have always been the

New Englanders like their strawberry shortcake made not out of cake, but out of biscuits, and at Durgin-Park only fresh strawberries are used.

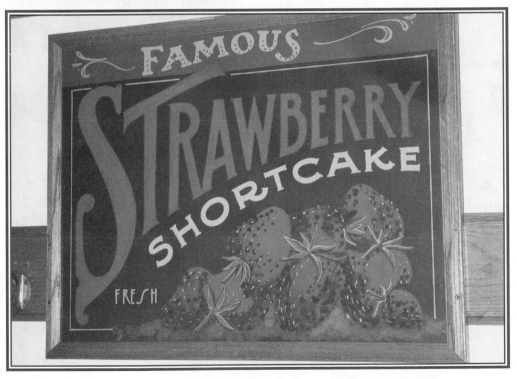

Lobster is as New England as are the Patriots.

lobster shacks, the neighborhood Portuguese and Greek and Hungarian and Italian joints that served homeland fare, and the honest urban eateries known for their square meals.

No place fits that last definition better than Durgin-Park. More than any other restaurant, its kitchen delineates the values of Yankee cooking—in its simplicity, its large portions, its obeisance to the old ways of doing things, its defiance of ceremony, and its embrace of downright dowdiness. We are quite sure that Boston baked beans, broiled schrod, Indian pudding, and coffee Jell-O will never enjoy the twenty minutes of fame that have been allotted such exotic regionalia as baked California goat cheese or blue corn pancakes. But that has always been just fine with the people of Durgin-Park, where the operative time frame is centuries rather than seasons.

• APPETIZERS •

BARBECUED CHICKEN WINGS

Long ago, eating chicken was a sign of prosperity and lobster was commoners' food. That hierarchy has reversed over the years, and now chicken is the economical dish. Ever since the 1960s when the Anchor Bar of Buffalo, New York, began offering wings as a munchable to go with drinks, the phenomenon of serving highly spiced drumettes has risen to the very top of America's snack consciousness. Durgin-Park's variation on the theme is sweet and tangy but not fiery hot.

½	cup soy sauce
½	cup pineapple juice
¼	cup vegetable oil
1	teaspoon dry mustard
1	tablespoon light brown sugar
2	teaspoons ground ginger
1	teaspoon garlic salt
⅓	teaspoon ground black pepper
3	to 4 pounds chicken wings

In a saucepan combine the soy sauce, pineapple juice, oil, mustard, brown sugar, ginger, garlic salt, and pepper. Bring to a boil and simmer for six minutes. Allow to cool completely. Pour the sauce over the chicken wings; marinate in the refrigerator for 3 hours, turning often. Preheat the oven to 425°F. Cook the wings on a baking sheet, skin side down for 20 minutes; turn and brush with the remaining marinade. Cook for 15 more minutes; serve immediately.

MAKES 4 TO 6 SERVINGS

COCKTAIL SAUCE

No big-night-on-the-town meal is complete without an appetizer of shrimp cocktail or bacon-wrapped scallops. The former demands traditional bright red cocktail sauce with a good whiplash of horseradish. This sauce is also suitable to accompany raw oysters or clams.

2	cups ketchup
¼	cup prepared horseradish
⅓	cup tomato juice
8	to 10 drops Tabasco sauce
5	to 6 drops Worcestershire sauce

In a bowl mix together the ketchup, horseradish, tomato juice, Tabasco sauce, and Worcestershire sauce. Chill.

MAKES ABOUT 2 ⅓ CUPS

FRIED CHICKEN FINGERS

Personally, we enjoy worrying chicken off the bone, but for those who want to concentrate entirely on eating (and drinking) without thinking about detours and delays caused by such extraneous things, chicken fingers are a suitable pop-in-the-mouth appetizer.

1	large egg
1	cup milk
1	cup fine bread crumbs
4	teaspoons onion powder
4	teaspoons garlic powder
2	teaspoons poultry seasoning
4	teaspoons ground white pepper
2	teaspoons paprika
1	pound fresh chicken tenders
½	cup flour

In a bowl mix together the egg and milk to make an egg wash. In a separate bowl combine the bread crumbs, onion and garlic powders, poultry seasoning, white pepper, and paprika. Dredge the chicken fingers in the flour, then the egg wash, then the bread crumb mixture. Deep fry until golden brown.

MAKES 4 SERVINGS

MINI CRAB CAKES

Most people associate crab cakes with the Mid-Atlantic states, but crabmeat is harvested in Maine, too; and it is popular all along the northeast coast—in salads, in toasted split-bun rolls, and as normal-size or mini crab cakes. While these are two-to-three-bite cakes that make fine hors d'oeuvres, there is no reason a half-dozen of them cannot be served as a main course.

2	*extra large eggs, slightly beaten*
⅓	*cup seasoned, dry bread crumbs*
2	*tablespoons minced parsley*
2	*tablespoons fresh lemon juice*
2	*tablespoons mayonnaise*
1	*tablespoon Worcestershire sauce*
4	*tablespoons minced chives*
	Salt and white pepper
3	*liberal dashes of hot red pepper sauce*
1	*pound fresh crabmeat, picked over for shells*
	Corn oil
	Lemon wedges

In a large mixing bowl combine the eggs, bread crumbs, parsley, lemon juice, mayonnaise, Worcestershire sauce, chives, salt and pepper (to taste), and pepper sauce. Mix thoroughly; then gently mix in the crab, keeping the crab pieces as large as possible. Place in a covered, plastic container and chill at least 8, and up to 24, hours. Stir the mixture occasionally to help the bread crumbs absorb the liquids. The mixture will be quite loose and will barely hold together during cooking.

In a 9-inch, heavy skillet, heat ½-inch oil over medium heat. Drop 5 teaspoon-sized dollops of crab mixture into the hot fat and cook 1 to 2 minutes. Turn the cakes over with a slotted spoon and repeat. The crab cakes should be the size of a half-dollar and cooked until golden brown. Drain on paper towels and serve with lemon wedges.

MAKES 8 SERVINGS

ONION RINGS

On Cape Ann, less than an hour north of Boston, deep-frying things is a fine art. Locally harvested clams are the most famous thing to fry; but the bubbling oil also yields every other sort of seafood worth battering. The best way to enjoy it is as part of a "platter," which means that the seafood is accompanied by—or completely covered with—great heaps of French fries and onion rings. Crisp, sweet Vidalia onions from Georgia make the best rings.

¾	*plus ¾ cup flour*
1	*tablespoon paprika*
	Salt and pepper
½	*tablespoon garlic powder*
2	*large eggs*
⅔	*cup water*
6	*to 8 large Vidalia onions, sliced ⅛-inch thick*

In a bowl combine ¾ cup of flour, the paprika, salt and pepper to taste, and garlic powder. In a separate bowl beat the eggs and combine with the water. Dredge the onion rings in the remaining ¾ cup plain flour, then the egg wash, and finally in the seasoned flour. Deep fry until golden brown.

MAKES 6 TO 8 SERVINGS

SCALLOPS WRAPPED IN BACON

We had never even thought of having an appetizer at Durgin-Park until last year when manager Seana Kelley suggested we precede our prime rib plates with a few scallops. We devoured a large plate of these utterly simple but deeply satisfying mouthfuls, and rich as they are, they only piqued our appetites for the several pounds of beef that soon arrived.

½   *pound bacon*
1   *pound fresh sea scallops*

Preheat the oven to 425°F. Cut the bacon in half, wrap the strips around the scallops, and pierce with a toothpick to hold the bacon. Bake for 8 to 10 minutes, turning once to brown the bacon.

MAKES 3 TO 4 SERVINGS

SHRIMP SCAMPI

Butter, shrimp, and garlic, with the taste of sherry wine, are an exquisite combination of ingredients. Serve this dish with sturdy bread for dipping in the savory juices.

½	cup butter
6	to 8 cloves fresh garlic
¼	cup sweet vermouth or sherry wine
¼	cup chicken stock
1	teaspoon white pepper
	Dash of Tabasco sauce
¼	cup freshly chopped parsley
12	large shrimp

Melt the butter in a sauté pan. Add the garlic, vermouth, chicken stock, white pepper, Tabasco sauce, and parsley and cook for 5 minutes until well blended. Add the shrimp and cook until firm. Be careful not to overcook.

MAKE 2 SERVINGS

DURGIN-PARK THROUGH THE YEARS

DURGIN-PARK GOT its name before the Civil War when two of its three owners were John Durgin and Eldredge Park. When they died, the third partner, John Chandler, was not inclined to change the formula. Chandler continued at the helm into the early twentieth century, when his descendants took over. In 1945 Chandler's family sold the restaurant to James Hallett, who ran it for fifty years. After Hallett died in 1977, his family sold it to the current owners, the Kelleys and Mike Solimando. That's basically three changes of ownership in two centuries!

In its earliest days Durgin-Park opened for business at 4:00 A.M., which is when the men of the Quincy Market began their day. Wearing their white coats and straw hats, they climbed up the stairs before dawn for breakfast, then returned mid-morning for a big hot meal. By noon, the tables were shared with local politicians, and when the butchers and produce sellers closed up shop mid-afternoon, they repaired to the pub at street level beneath Durgin-Park's dining room. Those who came to eat supper were known to wait for their tables down in the lobby, drink flagons of beer, and sing along with the player piano in the pub.

There are no reviews to tell us exactly what it was like to dine in this place 150 years ago (that was before the profession of restaurant reviewer existed!), but it seems apparent that it was

DURGIN, PARK & CO.,

EAST VIEW OF FANEUIL HALL MARKET.
1827

James Hallett, starting in the mid-twentieth century, who established the distinctive Durgin-Park personality that endures today. A strict man who had his own way of doing everything, he made sure all his employees, both in the kitchen and on the floor of the dining room, complied. Dissatisfied with the way local linen companies supplied him with tablecloths, he installed his own laundry on Durgin-Park's upper floor (using a crane to hoist the huge washing machines up from the street and into the window); to this day, the restaurant cleans all its own linen.

It was under Hallett's stewardship that the waitstaff became famous for being rude to customers. Overhearing one of his girls ask a group of people if everything was okay, Hallett is alleged to have taken her aside to reprimand her, telling her never to ask customers if everything was all right. "I serve the best food around," he said. "Of course everything's all right." One of Hallett's peculiarities was to insist that every customer be provided a separate check, so that if you were host of a party of six, you got six handwritten checks to settle. No wonder the waitresses got crabby! Under the Kelleys, the reputation of the waitstaff transformed from out-and-out insolence to an enjoyable kind of sass. It is not unusual today to see them smile and to actually inquire if a meal is to the customer's liking.

Like Tommy Ryan, James Hallett began in the market as a meat cutter;

some time after he came to Durgin-Park and took over the restaurant, his brother, "Babe" Hallett, became chef. Babe began working under Albert Savage, who had run the kitchen since the late nineteenth century; and Babe's first position was that of Chief Bean Man—the person in charge of the all-important task of soaking and baking the beans. Babe learned from Albert Savage, as Tommy Ryan learned from Babe, that so many of the restaurant's signature dishes—including the baked beans—are made according to recipes that have not changed in well over a hundred years.

Aside from transforming the service from mean to impudent, the Kelleys brought a number of other "adjustments" to the restaurant when they took over. While the culinary basics have remained the same, they added fried lobster to the kitchen's more familiar repertoire of boiled and sautéed. Pasta was put on the menu in the early 1990s in a tip of the hat to runners in the Boston Marathon, and sandwiches were offered (reluctantly) starting in 2001 for people without time or interest in a good hot meal.

One other thing the Kelleys did, for which all who remember the old days are immensely grateful, was to repaint the dining room. In the old days, the ugliness of the mustard-yellow walls was nearly as notorious as the impoliteness of the waitresses. Today, Durgin-Park's walls are an eye-easy ivory, decorated with attractive signs that advertise the kitchen's specialties and clippings from dozens of newspapers and magazines singing praises of the historic restaurant.

Despite such modernization, twenty-first century Durgin-Park wears a fine historical patina; simply to sit at its old communal tables, on the second story high above what used to be the city market, is to know what dining in Boston was like before all our grandfathers were born.

• SALADS •

CHICKEN SALAD

You will find salads on menus in every eat-in-the-rough restaurant down east of Providence. These are not the kinds of salads that are served in a bowl (although there would be no law against that) or in a splayed-open tomato. They are generally presented in the kind of long "split bun" that is unique to the region and frequently used to hold a hot dog—a thick roll of spongy white bread with a slit in the middle and two distinct sides that allow you to toast it on a well-buttered grill. While it is still warm, stuff the bun with a bit of lettuce, then pile in the salad. Serve with French fries or onion rings on the side and Whoopie Pie for dessert.

---

4   cups cooked white meat chicken, cubed
1   cup diced celery
⅔   cup mayonnaise
      Salt and pepper

In a bowl mix together the chicken, celery, and mayonnaise. And salt and pepper to taste. Spread between two slices of bread or on a roll for a sandwich. This salad may also be served on a bed of lettuce with crackers.

[Variation: Just before serving add 1 cup chilled pineapple tidbits or 1 cup green grapes.]

MAKES 4 SERVINGS

TUNA SALAD

Like the chicken salad and lobster salad, the tuna salad is not served in a bowl. Instead, this salad is served on the long "split bun" unique to the region. It can be served on a toasted bun with fries.

---

2   *(6-ounce) cans tuna, in water, drained and flaked*
¾   *cup finely chopped celery*
½   *cup mayonnaise*
     Salt and pepper

In a bowl mix together the tuna, celery, mayonnaise, and salt and pepper to taste. Spread between two pieces of bread or on a roll for a sandwich. This salad may also be served on a bed of lettuce with crackers.

MAKES 4 SERVINGS

LOBSTER SALAD

Similar to the chicken and tuna salads, the lobster salad is a healthy meal on a long "split bun" that is used to hold a hot dog. The bun is toasted on a well-buttered grill; while the bun is still warm, they stuff it full of lobster salad and serve it with fries.

3	cups cooked lobster meat
¾	cup finely chopped celery
¾	cup mayonnaise
	Salt and pepper

Cut the lobster meat into large bite-sized pieces. Place in a bowl and add celery, mayonnaise, and salt and pepper to taste. Spread between two slices of bread or on a roll for a sandwich. This salad may also be served on a bed of lettuce with crackers.

MAKES 4 SERVINGS

POTATO SALAD WITH MUSTARD DRESSING

Potato salad in New England is always rich and eggy—a staple at summertime picnics.

Salad:

5	pounds potatoes, preferably red-skinned, peeled and quartered
2	tablespoons cider vinegar
½	pound bacon (8 slices), cut into 1-inch pieces
¼	cup chopped onion
2	teaspoons celery seed
1½	teaspoons salt
1	teaspoon coarsely ground pepper

Dressing:

2	large eggs
1	cup sugar
⅓	cup yellow ballpark mustard
½	cup plus 2 tablespoons cider vinegar
1	cup less 2 tablespoons water
¾	cup chopped parsley, for garnish

Place the potatoes in a large pot with water to cover. Add the vinegar, cover, and bring to a boil over high heat. Lower the heat to medium and cook for 25 minutes, or until the potatoes are fork-tender. Drain very well and set aside to cool. Sauté the bacon until crisp. Remove the pan from the heat and set aside. Cube the potatoes and place them in a shallow pan (I use a 16-inch, round cake pan). Pour the bacon grease and bacon over the potatoes and add the onions, celery seed, salt, and pepper; toss lightly.

To make the dressing, beat the eggs slightly in a large saucepan. Add the sugar and blend. Beat in the mustard and then add the vinegar and water. Bring to a boil over medium-high heat and cook until the mixture starts to thicken, about 8 to 10 minutes, stirring frequently. The mixture will be quite runny. Pour the hot dressing over the potatoes and combine. Allow the salad to stand for 3 hours to absorb all the dressing, stirring occasionally. Stir in the parsley. Transfer to a serving bowl or storage container.

MAKES 12 SERVINGS

• BREADS •

BOSTON BROWN BREAD

California food writer Marion Cunningham, whose credits include the modern revision of Fannie Farmer's *Boston Cooking-School Cook Book,* once wrote a newspaper story titled "In Praise of Brown Food." It was about the consoling kitchen aromas of such drab-colored foods as baked beans, brown bread, and Indian pudding—a trio of dishes for which Durgin-Park is known.

Brown bread has been a Yankee kitchen fundamental since Pilgrim days when it was forbidden to cook on Sunday. On Saturdays, it was steamed in the wood-fired oven, along with baked beans, and served warm; cold baked beans and pieces of yesterday's brown bread became the Sabbath day meal.

⅓	cup rye or graham flour
⅓	cup all-purpose flour
⅓	cup yellow cornmeal
⅓	cup dry bread crumbs
1	teaspoon baking soda
½	teaspoon salt
1	cup buttermilk
½	cup dark molasses
⅓	cup dark raisins

In a medium bowl whisk together the flours, cornmeal, bread crumbs, baking soda, and salt. Stir in the buttermilk and molasses; do not overmix. Stir in the raisins. Coat a 1½ quart, metal steaming tin with vegetable oil cooking spray. Pour in the batter, run a knife or spatula through the batter to remove any air pockets, and cover tightly with a lid or foil. Place the mold on a rack (if you don't have a rack, canning jar rings work very well) in a deep pot with a tight-fitting lid. Add enough hot water to reach two-thirds up the sides of the mold; cover. Bring the water to a simmer and steam the bread for 2¼ hours on low heat. Check the pot from time to time to make sure the water is not boiling away. Remove the mold from the water and let it sit for 20 minutes; turn the bread out onto a rack to cool. To serve, cut in slices.

MAKES 1 LOAF

BREAD CRUMB STUFFING

Everybody is a stuffing chauvinist. We all assume that the stuffing we grew up eating, the one our mothers and grandmothers served, and the one we serve and our children will serve, is the only one there is, particularly when it comes to the all-important role of accompanying a serious turkey dinner.

3	cups bread crumbs
1	onion, minced
1	cup finely chopped celery
¾	cup butter, melted
1	teaspoon salt
¼	teaspoon pepper
½	teaspoon poultry seasoning or thyme, marjoram, or sage

Mix the bread crumbs, onion, celery, butter, salt, pepper and poultry seasoning with a fork.

MAKES ENOUGH STUFFING FOR A 10-POUND TURKEY

CORN BREAD I

Tommy Ryan credits the consistent excellence of Durgin-Park's corn bread to a woman called "Cornbread Helen," who had worked in the kitchen for twenty-five years when he arrived in 1960. "She gave me the recipe, and I didn't change a thing," he says. "Although she used to make it in big stone crocks. Today we put the batter into baking pans to cook it." How does the batter get into the pans from the big vat in which it is made? Baker Martin Gonzales scoops it out with his hands and splashes it straight into the baking pan.

¼	cup sugar, sifted
2	eggs, beaten
2	cups flour
3	teaspoons baking powder
¾	teaspoon salt
1	cup yellow cornmeal
1	tablespoon melted butter
1½	cups milk

Preheat the oven to 400°F. In a bowl mix the sugar and beaten eggs. In a separate bowl sift the flour, baking powder, and salt. Add the flour mixture to the egg mixture. Add the cornmeal, melted butter, and milk. Beat just enough to mix. Pour into a 8 x 12 x ½-inch-deep baking pan. Bake for about 30 minutes. This makes one pan full, which cuts into 20 squares.

MAKES 20 SERVINGS

CORN BREAD II

Thick, yellow squares of corn bread arrive at the table before every Durgin-Park meal. It is grainy and rough-textured, moist and slightly sweet. Sturdy enough to smear with butter, it is also ideal for crumbling onto the top of a dish of baked beans or a bowl of chowder. "The secret is mixing it by hand," Tommy Ryan says. "A machine makes it too fine, and you end up with cake."

3	cups all-purpose flour
2	cups yellow cornmeal
3	teaspoons salt
¾	cup sugar
8	teaspoons baking powder
2	large eggs
2½	cups milk

Preheat the oven to 375°F. In a large mixing bowl mix the flour, cornmeal, salt, sugar, and baking powder. Beat the eggs and add to the dry ingredients alternately with the milk. Mix by hand; do not use a mixer. Pour the mixture into an 11 x 13-inch baking dish and bake for 35 to 40 minutes. Cut into squares and serve hot.

MAKES 12 TO 14 SERVINGS

CORNMEAL PIE

As you might guess from the name of the recipe, cornmeal pie is a pie made of cornmeal. It is a good alternative to bread on the side of a main course that needs something grainy and tender for crumbling into gravy.

2	*cups chicken broth*
¼	*teaspoon salt*
	Scant ¼ teaspoon pepper
	Liberal pinch of ground nutmeg
½	*cup yellow (not stone-ground) cornmeal*
2	*tablespoons (¼ stick) butter*
4	*tablespoons grated Parmesan cheese*
	Paprika

In a deep medium saucepan combine the broth, salt, pepper, and nutmeg and bring to a boil. Add the cornmeal in a very slow stream, whisking constantly. Cover and cook over low heat, whisking now and then, for 15 minutes. Stir in the butter. Pour into a well-greased, 9-inch pie plate and smooth the top. Sprinkle with the Parmesan cheese and the paprika. Cover and chill the mixture for at least 30 minutes, or up to 12 hours.

Preheat the oven to 400°F. Bake the pie for 25 minutes, or until it is golden brown. Cut into wedges and serve hot.

MAKES 6 SERVINGS

THRIFT

THE COOKS OF New England did not invent the idea of thrifty cooking, but they have honed it to a fine point. Some of the best regional meals are made of leftovers, i.e., red flannel hash, which is a griddle-cooked meal created out of yesterday's boiled dinner, and Sunday baked-bean-on-brown-bread sandwiches, which are made from Saturday baked-bean-supper leftovers.

James Hallett, proprietor of Durgin-Park from 1945 to 1993, didn't like to waste anything. The story is told that early one morning he saw a waitress pouring out leftover coffee from the night before. "What are you doing with my coffee?" he asked her. She explained that no one wanted to drink yesterday's reheated brew, a point he couldn't argue. "Still," he thought, "there ought to be *something* we can do with it other than pour it out." And so he came up with the idea of making it into coffee-flavored Jell-O, a strangely dour dessert (p. 172) that has remained a staple of the Durgin-Park menu ever since.

Other frugal strategies that result in excellent food are the saving of leftover mashed potatoes to use in making fish cakes and transforming pieces of unordered roast beef into a wonderful, inexpensive meal called potted beef

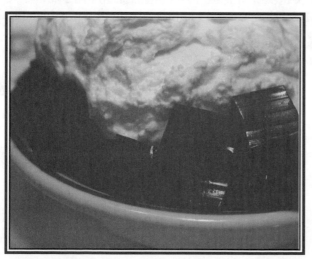

(p. 139), which is like ultra-tender and ultra-flavorful pot roast. Because chef Tommy Ryan cuts his own meat (cheaper than buying precut portions), the house-cured corned beef is especially delicious, the steaks are lovely, and the hamburgers (ground daily from steak trimmings) are the freshest and tastiest in town.

Even the thermodynamics of Durgin-Park reflect a waste-not attitude. The same basement boilers that provide heat for the four-story building are connected via old steam pipes to the huge soup pots in the kitchen, thus keeping the chowder warm, too.

But there are many aspects of Durgin-Park cookery in which perfectionism trumps parsimony. One is the use of water. For as long as anyone can remember, the restaurant has demurred the direct use of city tap water for tea and coffee in favor of more costly filtered water. The strawberries on strawberry shortcake are always fresh, even in the middle of winter when they have to be flown in at the daunting cost of thirty-plus dollars per flat (12 pints). And you can be sure that the shortcake will be topped with full-bodied, 36-percent-fat whipped cream.

Prudence is a virtue in the Yankee kitchen, but it does not trump the mandate to serve large portions of quality food.

CRANBERRY BREAD

Massachusetts is famous for its cranberries; down in Plymouth, travelers can visit Ocean Spray's Cranberry World, a kind of welcome center/museum that tells you everything there is to know about the tart fruit. In the gift shop, you'll have the opportunity to taste cranberry-based snacks, such as this sweet bread.

2	cups flour
½	teaspoon salt
1	teaspoon baking soda
1½	teaspoons baking powder
1	cup sugar
1	egg, slightly beaten
1	cup cranberries, chopped
1	cup nuts, chopped (optional)
	Juice and rind of 1 orange
2	tablespoons vegetable shortening
	Boiling water

Preheat the oven to 350°F. In a large bowl mix the flour, salt, baking soda, baking powder, and sugar. Blend in the egg, cranberries, and nuts, if using. Place in a measuring cup the orange juice, rind, and shortening and add enough of the boiling water to measure ¾ cup total. Add this to the dry mixture. Turn into a greased and floured, 10-inch tube pan. Bake for 50 to 60 minutes.

MAKES 1 LOAF

CREAMY BROILED GARLIC TOAST

When making a hearty fish stew, there's no better enhancement than a few chunks of creamy broiled garlic toast on the side. Eat them out of hand, or tear off bite-sized pieces for dunking and mopping the bowl.

1¼	cups mayonnaise
6	garlic cloves, finely minced
1	cup grated Parmesan cheese
¾	cup grated extra sharp Cheddar cheese
1½	tablespoons milk or cream
½	teaspoon paprika
¼	cup finely minced parsley
1	(20-inch) loaf French bread

Preheat the broiler; position the rack 6 inches from the heat. In a small bowl mix the mayonnaise, garlic, and Parmesan cheese. Combine the Cheddar cheese and milk or cream in a small saucepan and heat over medium-low heat until melted, stirring constantly so it doesn't scorch. Remove from the heat and whisk the mayonnaise mixture into the cheese mixture. Stir in the paprika and parsley. Cut the loaf in half lengthwise as for a hero sandwich, or cut it into individual slices. Arrange the bread on a baking sheet and toast lightly under the broiler until just golden. Spread the toasts generously with the cheese mixture, return to the oven, and broil 2 to 3 minutes, or until the cheese is bubbly and deep golden brown. Cut into serving pieces if the loaf was left whole and serve hot.

MAKES 8 SERVINGS

BEST NEW ENGLAND JOHNNYCAKE

When Durgin-Park was asked to come up with a recipe for johnnycakes (sometimes spelled jonnycakes), they found this little piece of antiquity from the *Model Cook Book* of 1885, noting that you should not try making it at home.

1	*quart buttermilk*
1	*teacup (6 ounces) flour*
⅓	*teacup (2 ounces) molasses*
	Pinch of salt
1	*teaspoon saleratus (baking soda)*
1	*egg*
	Indian meal

"To make this johnnycake," according to the *Model Cook Book* published in 1885, "take one quart of buttermilk, one teacup of flour, ⅓ of a teacupful of molasses, a little salt, one teaspoonful of saleratus [baking soda], one egg (beat, of course). Then stir in Indian meal, but be sure not to put in too much. Leave it thin, so thin that it will almost run. Bake in a tin in any oven, and tolerably quick. If it is not first-rate and light, it will be because you make it too thick with Indian meal. Some prefer it without the molasses."

MAKES 1 SERVING

PUMPKIN BREAD

New England food expert Brooke Dojny calls this the "quintessentially autumn-in-New-England quick bread."

⅔	cup margarine
2⅔	cups sugar
4	eggs
1	can pumpkin
⅔	cup water
3⅓	cups flour
½	teaspoon baking powder
2	teaspoons baking soda
1½	teaspoons salt
1	teaspoon ground cinnamon
1	teaspoon ground cloves
⅔	cup chopped walnuts
⅔	cup raisins

Preheat the oven to 350°F. Cream the margarine and sugar. Add the eggs, pumpkin, and water. In a separate bowl sift the flour, baking powder, baking soda, salt, cinnamon, and cloves and add to the pumpkin mixture. Stir in the nuts and raisins. Turn into two 9-inch greased loaf pans. Bake for 1 hour.

MAKES 2 LOAVES

VERMONT GRAHAM BREAD

Graham flour, from which graham crackers are made, is in fact nothing other than whole wheat flour. A little over a hundred years ago, it became the cause célèbre of Connecticut resident Reverend Sylvester Graham, who was the first figure in popular culture to inveigh against the evils of white bread. Graham so believed in the goodness of eating well that he established a vegetarian utopian community near Boston called Fruitland, where his followers ate only roots, fruits, and whole grains. What with its sour cream and buttermilk, this bread recipe would no doubt have piqued the Reverend Graham (a strict vegan), but for those of us who choose to live devil-may-care, it makes a scrumptious loaf.

1½	*cups sour milk or buttermilk*
2	*tablespoons sour cream or melted butter*
⅔	*cup molasses and maple syrup (half of each or alone)*
2	*teaspoons baking soda*
½	*teaspoon salt*
1⅓	*cups graham flour*
1⅓	*cups flour, sifted*
	Raisins (optional)

Preheat the oven to 350°F. Mix together the sour milk, sour cream, molasses, baking soda, salt, flours, and raisins, if using. Bake in a greased 6 x 8-inch loaf pan for 45 to 50 minutes.

MAKES 1 LOAF

• SOUPS •

BAKED BEAN SOUP I

Baked beans are a dish by which Boston is known, and there isn't anything else on the Durgin-Park menu that gets chef Tommy Ryan more worked up than a discussion of what makes a real Boston baked bean. In his kitchen the beans are cooked throughout the week the old-fashioned way in real bean pots, and there are almost always plenty left over. The easiest thing to do with leftover baked beans is to mash them a bit and use them as the ingredient for a brown bread sandwich. But one of the most delicious alternatives is to transform them into soup. Here are three ways to do it.

3	*cups baked beans*
1	*quart water or beef stock*
2	*tablespoons minced onion*
2	*to 3 tablespoons finely chopped celery*
1	*teaspoon instant coffee (optional)*
4	*uncooked franks, or ¼ cup diced salt pork or hard sausage*
2	*tablespoons sherry*
1	*lemon, sliced*
2	*hard-cooked eggs, finely chopped*

Preheat the oven to 200°F. In a blender combine the beans, water or stock, onion, and celery, blending until smooth. Pour this resulting purée into an ovenproof dish and simmer in the oven on low heat (200°F) for about 30 minutes, adding a little liquid only if it seems too thick. (One Vermont cook adds a teaspoon of instant coffee to give her soup a deeper color; the flavor blends into the point of mystery.) Fry the pork (whatever you choose) until crisp. (If using sausage, cut it into small pieces.) Raise the oven temperature to 350°F; add the meat to the soup and continue to heat, about 10 minutes. Add the sherry just before ladling the soup into hot dishes. Put a lemon slice in each serving and sprinkle in bits of the chopped egg.

MAKES 6 SERVINGS

BAKED BEAN SOUP II

2	cups cold baked beans
2	medium-sized onions, minced
½	clove garlic, finely chopped
4	cups cold water
2	cups canned tomatoes
2	tablespoons flour
2	tablespoons butter
	Salt and freshly ground black pepper

Preheat the oven to 300°F. Place the beans, onions, garlic, and water in a bean pot and simmer in the oven for about 30 minutes. Put the tomatoes through an electric blender or food mill, heat, and add to the bean mixture. In a bowl mix the flour and butter together and add a little of the hot soup. Return all to the pot and cook, stirring occasionally, until the soup thickens. Season with the salt and pepper to taste.

MAKES 6 SERVINGS

BAKED BEAN SOUP III

3   cups cold baked beans

3   pints water

2   small onions, sliced

2   ribs celery, chopped

1½   cups stewed and strained tomatoes

2   tablespoons chili sauce

     Salt and pepper

2   tablespoons butter

2   tablespoons flour

Preheat the oven to 300°F. Put the baked beans, water, onions, and celery into a bean pot. Simmer for 30 minutes in the oven. Remove the beans from the oven and put them through a sieve. Add the tomatoes and chili sauce; season to taste with the salt and pepper. Cook the flour and butter in a saucepan over low heat until thoroughly mixed and add to the beans to bind them together.

MAKES 8 SERVINGS

CHICKEN SOUP

Note that this recipe calls for a large chicken, as close as possible to what butchers used to sell as a stewing hen. While too tough for eating in parts, a big old fowl has a deeper flavor that gives this soup the power to make the sick well and the anxious serene.

1	*(4- to 6-pound) whole chicken*
1	*cup chicken base*
6	*teaspoons white pepper*
6	*teaspoons celery salt*
6	*to 8 ribs celery, chopped*
4	*to 6 carrots, chopped*
	Rice or noodles, for serving

Cut the chicken into quarters; place in a stockpot. Cover it with water and add the chicken base, white pepper, and celery salt. Boil the meat until it is tender and starts to fall off the bones. Remove the chicken from the stock and cool before removing the meat from the bones. Cut or dice the meat. Bring the chicken stock to a boil. Add the meat, carrots, and celery to the stock and boil until the vegetables are tender, about 10 minutes. Reduce the heat and add cooked rice or noodles. Simmer for a few minutes before serving.

MAKES ABOUT 3 QUARTS

CREAM OF BROCCOLI SOUP

For the many people who don't like broccoli, it's the texture of the stalk that is often the trip wire for aversion. If that's the case, this soup might be just the thing to convert them, for its broccoli is transformed into rich, green cream. If, on the other hand, it's the flavor of broccoli that's the stumbling block, forget about it: this soup radiates vegetable taste.

3	bunches broccoli
6	ribs celery
8	ounces chicken base
6	teaspoons white pepper
6	teaspoons celery salt
½	cup butter
½	cup flour
1	quart heavy cream

Chop the broccoli and finely dice the celery. Place the broccoli and celery in a stockpot and cover with cold water. Bring to a boil; add the chicken base, white pepper, and celery salt. Reduce the heat and simmer until the broccoli is tender, about 10 minutes. In a small pan make a roux with the butter and flour; cook for 10 minutes. Strain the broccoli and mash; add it back to the stock along with the roux and the heavy cream.

MAKES 3 TO 4 QUARTS

HAM AND PEA SOUP

Smoked ham, infused with the flavor of maple syrup, is a Northern New England delicacy. If you get one of these smokehouse hams and eat it down to the bone, you then have the wherewithal to prepare one of the best hearty soups. Serve it with crunchy croutons piled on top.

2	cups (1 pound) dried split peas
3	quarts plus 1 quart water
1	large onion, minced
4	ribs celery, minced
2	carrots, minced
1	large clove garlic, minced
2	tablespoons butter
1	ham bone, or ½ pound ham pieces, finely chopped
1½	quarts chicken broth
1	medium onion, left whole and studded with 3 whole cloves
1	teaspoon ground black pepper

Cover the peas with the 3 quarts of water and soak overnight. The next day drain the peas and return them to the pot. Sauté the onion, celery, carrots, and garlic in the butter for 2 to 3 minutes; add the vegetables to the pot with the soaked peas. Add the ham bone, broth, the remaining 1 quart water, and the whole onion. Cover, and bring to a boil. Reduce the heat and simmer, stirring occasionally, for 1½ hours, or until the peas are tender and the soup is thickened. Remove the ham bone and the whole onion. Chop any meat from the bone and return the meat to the soup. Discard the bone and onion. Bring the soup to a boil and add salt and pepper to taste.

MAKES 8 SERVINGS

PURÉE OF SPLIT PEA SOUP

You don't need a big old ham bone to make split pea soup—just a leftover piece or two plus some salt pork.

1	cup yellow split peas
1½	cups green split peas
16	cups cold water
¼	pound salt pork, cut in pieces
1	small piece leftover ham, cut in pieces
2	ribs celery, diced
1	carrot, scraped and sliced
1	onion, sliced
¼	teaspoon pepper
1	teaspoon Worcestershire sauce
1	clove garlic (optional)
3	tablespoons flour
3	medium-sized potatoes, peeled and sliced
1½	cups light cream, scalded

Soak the peas in water overnight; drain, add the cold water, bring to a boil, and simmer for 30 minutes. Sauté the salt pork; add the ham, celery, onion, carrot, pepper, Worcestershire sauce, and garlic. Shake in the flour and continue to sauté for 15 minutes, stirring constantly. Combine with the peas; add the potatoes, simmer 2 hours longer, and then strain through purée strainer. (If the soup is too thick, add boiling water.) Before serving add cream, heat to boiling, season, and serve with Johnnycake (page 34).

MAKES 10 TO 12 SERVINGS

READING MENUS

SOME THINGS ABOUT the Durgin-Park menu never change. As far back as records show, the front has always featured a woodcut image of the east view of Faneuil Hall Market in 1827 and, below that, the words *Market Dining Rooms*. Seventy-five years ago, the catchphrase on the front was *"Where Your Grandfather Dined."* Sometime in the mid-twentieth century, that was changed to *"Your grandfather and perhaps your great-grandfather dined with us, too!"* and to that boast was added the incontrovertible claim, *"Established before you were born."* Relatively recent menus also inform diners that the restaurant is located in the shadow of Faneuil Hall, "which was deeded to the town of Boston by Peter Faneuil in 1742 for use as the Town Hall, affectionately called the 'Cradle of Liberty.'"

Reading the inside of the menu is a fascinating study not only of changing taste in food, but of inflation. In 1927 a slice of Durgin-Park roast prime rib of beef was listed at fifty-five cents, including bread and butter and boiled or mashed potato. In 1960 the prime rib sold for $3.75—the most expensive dish in the house. Menus from the early 1990s show the "Durgin Cut" prime rib (that's the jumbo one) going for $15.95; today its price is $21.95.

Some of the eternal house specialties include lobster, roast beef, fish cakes, baked beans (listed only recently as *Boston* baked beans to drive

DINNER BILL
PLEASE PAY CASHIER AT DESK

Clams			
	Little Necks, half doz.	25	Clam Cocktail ... 30

Soup and Chowder			
	Beef Soup ... 20	Clam Chowder (Mon., Wed. and Sat.) ..20
	Chicken Soup ... 20	Fish Chowder (Tues., Thurs. and Fri.) ..20
	Mutton Broth ... 20	
	Tomato ... 20	

Fish			
	Fried Cods' Tongues ... 35	Fried Cod ... 35
	Salt Cod and Beets (Wed. and Sat.) .. 35	Fried Clams ... 45
	Cod and Cream (Tuesday and Friday) . 35	Fried Halibut ... 50
	Boiled Halibut, Egg Sauce (Friday) 50	Broiled Halibut ... 50
		Broiled Scrod ... 40

Broiled Chicken Live Lobster, French Fried Potatoes 1.50
Broiled Live Lobster and French Fried Potatoes.................2.00
Fried Clams and French Fried Potatoes 50

SPECIAL	Broiled Fresh Mackerel	50
	Broiled Halibut	50
Dishes served this day	Broiled Swordfish	60
	Soft Shell Crabs (Fried)	65
	Plain Lobster and Lettuce	1.25
	Fried Sausages, Apple Sauce	50

	Roast Chicken, half, Cranberry Sauce	85
	Roast Spring Lamb, Mint Sauce	65
	Roast Rib of Beef	
Roasts	Roast Sirloin of Beef	75
	Roast Ham and Spinach	50
	Roast Pork, Apple Sauce	55
	Roast Stuffed Veal	50
	Fried Calf's Liver and Bacon	60
	Corned Beef and Spinach or String Beans	45
	Breast of Lamb Tomato Sauce Tues. & Thur.	35
	Curry of Veal with Rice, Mon. & Wed.	35
	Imported Frankfurts and Beans or Potato Salad	40
	P. & C. Imported Sardines and Potato Salad	60
	California Sardines and Potato Salad	40

home the point that they are not like beans anywhere else), and baked Indian pudding. There has always been an all-vegetable meal available, known in the 1920s simply as "Vegetable Dinner" (forty cents) and including a choice from among *twenty-three* different items: new cabbage, spinach, sliced new onions, boiled onions, fried onions, carrots, new green peas, string beans, lettuce, green corn (single ear), shell beans, succotash, turnips, beets, stewed tomatoes, coleslaw (listed on one menu as "cold slaw"), plain fried potatoes, French-fried potatoes, lyonnaise potatoes, hash brown potatoes, fried sweet potatoes, griddled sweet potatoes, and a boiled sweet potato! God bless a menu with multiple potato choices. Today's vegetable dinner is known as "Bale of Hay" ($7.95) and includes four different vegetables plus a potato.

Menus have always made a point of alerting guests to the fact that Durgin-Park coffee is available and on sale at the cashier's desk (forty-five cents per pound in 1927), and that only filtered water is used to make it. The current menu says, "No splitting orders, please." Seventy-five years ago, it said, "ten cents extra charge for one order served to two persons."

What is most amazing about the early twentieth-century menus is how many different items were available. In addition to the twenty-three vegetables, there were *ten* different puddings for dessert—Boston, Indian, tapioca, apple tapioca, baked rice, boiled rice, baked plum, bread and butter, blueberry, and peach, each selling for either ten or fifteen cents per serving.

	Cream Cheese	10	with Toasted Crackers		20
	Camembert Cheese and Toasted Crackers				20
	Imported Roquefort Cheese and Toasted Crackers				25
Cake	Silver 10	Sponge 10	Raisin 10		Chocolate 10
Sauce	Apple Sauce.................... 10		Stewed Prunes		10
	Cranberry Sauce..................... 10		Preserved Fresh Figs		10
	Chili Sauce 5		With Cream		15
Drinks	Cider Jelly 10				
	Cocoa 10		Milk, per Glass		5
	Tea or Coffee...................... 10		Light Cream, per Glass		15

Not responsible for hats and coats or any articles left in our dining rooms
Open 6 A.M. until 7.15 P.M. Closed Sundays and Holidays
Telephone, Richmond 0416

The dessert menu also listed six kinds of pie (including green apple), four different cakes—silver, sponge, raisin, chocolate, and sixteen different cigars, ranging from the eight-cent Noble to the thirty-cent La Corona Perfecto. In the section devoted to breakfast (no longer available), eggs could be ordered boiled, fried, scrambled, or dropped on toast, sided by a rasher of bacon, fish cakes, or broiled honeycomb tripe.

CIGARS

La Corona, Perfecto .	30c. straight	
E. & E. Special Seleccion .	15c. straight	
7-20-4	13c., 2 for 25c.	3 for 35c.
Overland, Perfecto .	13c., 2 for 25c.	3 for 35c.
J. A.	13c., 2 for 25c.	3 for 35c.
Waitt & Bond, Blackstone .	13c., 2 for 25c.	3 for 35c.
E. & E., Rockefellers . .	13c., 2 for 25c.	3 for 35c.
Elcho . . .	13c., 2 for 25c.	3 for 35c.
Harvard . . .	13c., 2 for 25c.	3 for 35c.
M. C. A. . . .	13c., 2 for 25c.	3 for 35c.
Kilby . . .	13c., 2 for 25c.	3 for 35c.
El Producto . .	10c. straight	
El Producto . .	10c. straight	
Peter Schuyler . .	10c. straight	
El Roitan . .		
Noble . . .	8c., 2 for 15c.	

Some other items no longer found on the menu of Durgin-Park (nor of many other restaurants) are mutton broth, fried cods' tongues, gridironed tomatoes, cream served by the glass to drink, Burkhardt beer, Pureoxia ginger ale, and such vanished brands of cigarettes as Murad, Melachrino, Fatima, and Perfection.

The old phone number was simply Richmond 0416. Today's menu directs customers to www.durgin-park.com.

TURKEY VEGETABLE SOUP

For most of us, this is an especially good soup to have two days after Thanksgiving—after the celebration meal and after having hot turkey sandwiches the first day. The turkey carcass that remains is a perfect soup-making opportunity. At Durgin-Park, where a couple of dozen fresh turkeys are cooked every week of the year, the kitchen always has the essential makings for this strapping soup.

1	*roasted turkey carcass, plus up to 4 cups leftover turkey meat cut into 1-inch cubes*
2	*tablespoons vegetable oil*
12	*cups water*
2	*plus 4 large carrots, chopped*
2	*plus 2 celery ribs, chopped*
1	*plus 1 large onion, chopped*
6	*sprigs plus ¼ cup chopped fresh parsley*
1	*teaspoon dried thyme*
2	*bay leaves*
2	*teaspoons salt*
½	*teaspoon pepper*
4	*tablespoons butter*
3	*large red potatoes (about 1 pound), cut into 2-inch chunks*
1	*teaspoon dried marjoram*

Using a heavy cleaver or knife, chop the carcass into large pieces. In a stockpot heat the oil. Add the carcass pieces and cook over moderately high heat, turning often, until the pieces are browned, about 10 minutes. Add the water, making sure it covers the carcass pieces. Add the 2 chopped carrots, 2 chopped celery ribs, and 1 chopped onion. Bring to a simmer; skim off any foam that rises to the top. Add the 6 parsley sprigs, thyme, bay leaves, salt, and pepper. Simmer for at least 2 to 4 hours. Strain the broth into a large bowl, discarding the carcass and vegetables. In a clean stockpot melt the butter. Add the remaining 4 chopped carrots, 2 chopped celery ribs, and 1 chopped onion. Cook covered over moderate heat, stirring occasionally, until the vegetables are softened, about 10 minutes. Add the potatoes, turkey broth, chopped parsley, and marjoram and bring to a boil. Reduce the heat and simmer partially covered for 30 to 40 minutes. Add the cubed turkey and heat through, about 5 minutes.

MAKES ABOUT 4 QUARTS

VEGETABLE SOUP

Vegetable soup is simplicity itself, a vehicle for the sweet flavors of vegetables to coalesce. While it is perfectly fine to use canned beef stock, it is 100 percent better if you have stock you've made by boiling beef bones with all their marrow flavor.

1	medium head cabbage
6	medium carrots
2	medium onions
8	ribs celery
1	(3-pound) can Italian tomatoes
6	ounces beef stock
6	teaspoons celery salt
6	teaspoons ground pepper
6	bay leaves

Cut the cabbage, carrots, onions, celery, and tomatoes into bite-sized pieces. Place the vegetables in a stockpot and cover them with water. Add the beef base, celery salt, pepper, and bay leaves. Bring to a boil. Reduce the heat and simmer for 1 hour, or until the vegetables are tender.

MAKES 4 QUARTS

VEGETABLE BEEF SOUP

Like James Hallett, the former proprietor, Durgin-Park chef Tommy Ryan started his career as a meat man, and so he knows his way with a carving knife. As has always been the case, the restaurant buys no precut steaks or chops; instead, the kitchen gets large sections of "swinging beef" that are butchered as needed into everything from prime rib to hamburger. From the "leftovers" come the bones that are used to give this vegetable soup its deep, beefy flavor.

4	pounds beef chine (soup bone)
10	cups water
½	cup diced onion
¼	cup diced carrots
½	head cabbage, chopped
¼	cup diced celery
2	cups diced, ripe tomatoes
2	teaspoons salt
1	bay leaf

In a large pot, put the soup bone in cold water, bring to a boil, and cook it until the meat falls from the bone. Cool. Remove the fat and bones. Cut the meat into small cubes and put back in the pot along with the onion, carrots, cabbage, celery, and tomatoes. Season with the salt and bay leaf. Bring to a boil and simmer until the vegetables are tender, about 1 hour.

MAKES APPROXIMATELY 2½ QUARTS

CORN CHOWDER

Soup, stew, and chowder have three very different meanings in the Yankee kitchen. A soup is generally built around vegetables. A stew, traditionally, was little more than cream, butter, and large pieces of seafood, such as lobster and oysters. (Today, New England stews may include vegetables and broth or stock.) A chowder is a hearty meal. Nowadays, chowder is virtually synonymous with seafood. Inland chowders made with corn and salt pork, however, are a farmhouse tradition and are served with common crackers (page 55) on the side.

4	tablespoons diced salt pork
1	tablespoon plus 3 tablespoons butter
1	medium onion, sliced
3	potatoes, peeled and finely diced
2	cups chicken stock
2	cups fresh or frozen corn
4	cups milk
	Salt and pepper
1	cup heavy cream

Fry the salt pork in 1 tablespoon butter; remove the pieces when crispy and reserve. Add the onion to the fat and sauté until golden. Add the potatoes and chicken stock and cook slowly until soft, about 10 minutes. Add the corn and milk, lower the heat, and simmer until the corn is tender, about 5 minutes. Add the salt and pepper to taste. Bring the mixture to a boil and remove from the heat. Add the cream and the remaining 3 tablespoons butter. Stir well. Float the pork pieces on top.

MAKES 6 SERVINGS

CLAM CHOWDER

We do not recognize Rhode Island clam chowder," declares chef Tommy Ryan. "They've got tomatoes in it." At this, he shrugs as if there is no more to say: end of discussion, point proved. New England clam chowder as made at Durgin-Park contains no tomatoes; in fact, it contains no vegetables at all except for potatoes. Its character is based on the simple commingling of ocean-sweet clams and dairy-rich half-and-half with a thick ribbon of melted butter to tie the two together.

4	pounds chopped clams
46	ounces clam juice
6	teaspoons celery salt
6	teaspoons white pepper
6	teaspoons Worcestershire sauce
3	teaspoons Tabasco sauce
4	to 6 whole potatoes
1	pound butter
1	pound flour
1	quart half-and-half

Place the clams and clam juice in a stockpot. Add the celery salt, white pepper, Worcestershire sauce, and Tabasco sauce. Peel and dice the potatoes. Add to the clams. Bring to a boil, lower the heat to simmer, and cook slowly. In a small saucepan melt the butter. Add the flour to make a white roux. Cook for 15 to 20 minutes on low heat. Whisk the roux into the clam mixture, and add the half-and-half. Cook slowly to blend all the ingredients.

MAKES 4 TO 6 SERVINGS

FISH CHOWDER

While clam chowder is a nearly everyday dish in many New England restaurants, fish chowder is the traditional Friday special. With a loaf of bread or plenty of oyster crackers, it is a self-sufficient meal.

4	pounds cod or pollock
1	cup clam juice or fish stock
6	teaspoons celery salt
6	teaspoons white pepper
4	teaspoons Worcestershire sauce
6	bay leaves
½	cup butter
6	to 8 ribs celery, chopped
1	medium onion, chopped
1	quart half-and-half

In a stockpot place the fish, stock, celery salt, white pepper, Worcestershire sauce, and bay leaves. Cover with water. Bring to a boil, and then lower the heat to simmer. In a skillet melt the butter and sauté the celery and onion before adding them to the fish stock; bring to a boil. Add the half-and-half and simmer before serving.

MAKES 12 SERVINGS

SCALLOP CHOWDER

The Boston pronunciation of *scallop* is skollup, and there are two different kinds. Bay scallops are the tiny ones, harvested close to the shore. Sea scallops are larger, brought up from the deeper ocean waters. Both are available fresh in cold weather; but because scallops freeze well, you can generally get them year-round. For chowder, the bigger sea scallops are what you want.

The "common crackers" called for in this recipe are old-fashioned store crackers that used to be kept in barrels. They are carried by many gourmet specialty stores or are available directly from the source, the Vermont Country Store (www.vermontcountrystore.com), which produces them according to the original 1828 recipe.

4	*tablespoons butter*
2	*small onions, sliced*
1	*pint scallops, cut in pieces*
2	*cups boiling water*
1	*cup diced potatoes*
4	*cups milk, scalded*
	Salt and pepper
	Common crackers, split and toasted

In a large saucepan melt the butter and lightly brown the onions. Remove the onions. Cook the scallops in the butter for 5 minutes. Add the boiling water, the browned onions, and the potatoes; simmer for 30 minutes. Add the scalded milk, and simmer for 15 minutes longer. Season with the salt and pepper to taste. Serve with the crackers.

MAKES 5 SERVINGS

BEAN POT STEW

While it is, of course, possible to make this stew in a regular ovenproof casserole dish, it's much more fun to make and serve in a Durgin-Park bean pot. The restaurant kitchen goes through hundreds of bean pots every year . . . and sells them in various sizes downstairs at the cash register.

1	pound beef (bottom round), cut in cubes
1	onion, chopped
2	tablespoons fat
2	small carrots, sliced
1	small turnip, sliced
1	cup peas, fresh or canned
4	tablespoons rolled oats
1	teaspoon salt
	Pepper
3	potatoes, cubed

Preheat the oven to 350°F. Brown the beef and onion in the fat; add the carrots, turnip, and peas. Turn into a greased bean pot or casserole. Add the rolled oats, salt, and pepper to taste. Cover with water and bake for 4 hours. Add the potatoes the last hour of cooking.

MAKES 4 SERVINGS

OPPOSITE PAGE: *As a tribute to his son who was killed in the Vietnam war, former proprietor James Hallett put the poem "Just a Boy" on the back of the Durgin-Park menu, and it has appeared there for three decades.*

Just a Boy...

Got to understand the lad —
　　He's not eager to be bad;
If the right he always knew,
　　He would be as old as you.
Were he now exceeding wise.
　　He'd be just about your size;
When he does things that annoy,
　　Don't forget — he's just a boy.

　　　　Could he know and understand,
　　　　　　He would need no guiding hand;
　　　　But he's young and hasn't learned
　　　　　　How life's corners must be turned.
　　　　Doesn't know from day to day
　　　　　　There is more to life than play.
　　　　More to face than selfish joy.
　　　　　　Don't forget — he's just a boy.

Being just a boy he'll do
　　Much you will not want him to;
He'll be careless of his ways,
　　Have his disobedient days.
Wilful, wild and headstrong, too,
　　He'll need guidance kind and true;
Things of value he'll destroy,
　　But reflect — he's just a a boy.

　　　　Just a boy who needs a friend,
　　　　　　Patient, kindly to the end;
　　　　Needs a father who will show
　　　　　　Him the things he wants to know,
　　　　Take him with you when you walk,
　　　　　　Listen when he wants to talk,
　　　　His companionship enjoy,
　　　　　　Don't forget — he's just a boy.

BEEF STEW

The clear division between soups and main courses that exists in much of the nation does not apply to New England cookery. Usually, what Yankees call a stew is in fact more of a soup, and like many chowders, you can eat it with either a spoon or a fork. This recipe for beef stew is a hearty meal . . . but serve it in a soup bowl, with a spoon and a fork.

4	*pounds stew beef*
	Flour for dredging
2	*tablespoons celery salt*
2	*tablespoons white pepper*
6	*bay leaves*
5	*ounces A-1 sauce*
10	*ounces beef stock*
1	*(3-pound) can stewed tomatoes*
6	*to 8 potatoes*
6	*to 8 carrots*
1	*rib celery*
2	*small onions*
1	*turnip*

Preheat the oven to 400°F. Dredge the stew beef in the flour and place it in a roasting pan. Roast for 30 to 35 minutes or until the beef is browned. Remove the beef from the pan and put it in a large stockpot. Cover the beef with water; add the celery salt, white pepper, bay leaves, A-1 sauce, beef base, and tomatoes. Simmer for one hour. Peel the vegetables, cut into bite-sized pieces, and add to the pot. Simmer for an additional hour. Remove from the heat; let the soup rest for 5 to 10 minutes before serving.

MAKES 8 TO 10 SERVINGS

CARL BARRON'S BEEF STEW

Carl Barron and his beloved wife, Ruth, of Cambridge, Massachusetts, have been loyal patrons of Durgin-Park for the past eighty years. Throughout this time they have brought people from around the globe to dine at Durgin-Park. The Barrons' children, grandchildren, the employees of his company (Putnam Furniture Leasing), and many local dignitaries have enjoyed Carl's fond memories of this restaurant throughout his decades as a "regular."

This beef stew recipe is still made by Carl and enjoyed by many of his friends. Durgin-Park is grateful to be his "top pick" in Boston.

2	to 2½ pounds sirloin tips
3	meaty beef bones
½	pound peeled baby carrots
2	peeled white potatoes, cut into quarters
3	ribs celery with as many leaves as possible, cut into 1-inch lengths
	Black pepper
½	(14-ounce) bottle of ketchup
⅔	cup barley
1	(8-ounce) can cooked mushrooms
1	(8-ounce) can green peas (optional)

Preheat the oven to 350°F. In a medium to large heavy pot, combine the sirloin tips, beef bones, carrots, and potatoes. Cut the celery into 1-inch lengths, and sprinkle over top of contents. Add black pepper to taste. Cover the meat and vegetables with the ketchup. Add sufficient water to not quite cover the entire contents. Cover and put in the oven for approximately 3 hours. Stir the contents about once every hour. After about 2½ hours, add the barley, mushrooms, and, if you like them, green peas. Stir again and cook for about 30 minutes more. The stew is ready when the meat peels off the bones.

MAKES 10 TO 12 SERVINGS

LAMB STEW

Traditional New England cookbooks are filled with recipes for stew: seafood, meat, and all-vegetable. These one-dish meals are thrifty and filling and will likely provide leftovers for a couple of days. The popularity of lamb on most regional menus has waned (except at Greek-run diners), but it's always been a staple at Durgin-Park.

3	*pounds lean lamb shoulder (free of bone), cut into 2-inch pieces*
	Flour
	Salt and pepper
	Dry mustard
4	*tablespoons butter*
4	*tablespoons grated onion*
	Boiling water to cover the lamb
3	*large onions, sliced*
2	*carrots, diced*
4	*potatoes, diced*
6	*ribs celery, chopped*

Use a cast iron kettle or a deep skillet. Dredge the lamb in the flour, seasoned with the salt, pepper, and dry mustard. Melt the butter; add the grated onion and meat and cook over medium heat until well browned. Stir in the water; cover and simmer for 30 minutes. Add the sliced onions, carrots, potatoes, celery, and more salt, if needed. Remove the cover and simmer for 1 hour. Check the liquid; add water if needed, but there should not be excess liquid. Cook the meat until tender.

MAKES 10 TO 12 SERVINGS

OVEN-BAKED LAMB STEW

Perhaps because of its climate, but also because of its frugal nature, New England has always favored stick-to-the-rib dishes that stretch out a small supply of meat to serve large numbers of people. Durgin-Park offered us three different recipes for lamb stew, a cold-weather supper for those in search of comfort food with a vintage taste.

⅓	*cup flour*
2	*teaspoons salt*
½	*teaspoon pepper*
1	*teaspoon brown sugar*
1	*pound lamb shoulder, boned and cut into 1-inch pieces*
½	*cup butter*
1	*large onion, finely chopped, plus 2 small onions, chopped*
1	*cup finely chopped celery*
2	*cups peeled, seeded, and chopped tomatoes*
2	*cups chicken stock*
2	*cups chopped carrots*
1	*cup heavy cream*
2	*egg yolks, beaten*
1	*cup cooked peas*
2	*tablespoons chopped parsley*

Preheat the oven to 350°F. In a bowl mix together the flour, salt, pepper, and brown sugar. Dredge the lamb in the seasoned flour. In a skillet sauté the meat in the butter until it is browned on all sides; add the chopped onion, celery, and tomatoes, and sauté for 10 minutes. Remove all to a greased baking dish. Add the chicken stock, the 2 small onions, and carrots. Cover; bake for 1½ hours. Liquid should be reduced considerably. Mix the cream with the beaten yolks and add to the meat, along with the peas. Sprinkle parsley on top and serve.

MAKES 6 TO 8 SERVINGS

LOBSTER STEW, CASCO BAY

Casco Bay in southern Maine is demarcated by Cape Elizabeth to the west and Cape Small to the east. It has been a seaport used by commercial fishermen since Colonial days, now home to nearly one hundred trawlers and the place lobstermen bring their pots ashore. Lobster stew is a shellfish lover's delight, full of meat and flavored with clam broth.

5	pounds lobster, boiled
5	tablespoons butter
5	cups top milk (half milk and half cream)
2	cups clam broth
	Salt
	Paprika
	Cayenne

Remove the meat from the shell and dice. Sauté in the butter for 3 or 4 minutes. Stir in the top milk and clam broth. Simmer for about 6 minutes. Season to taste with the salt and paprika and add a sprinkle of cayenne.

MAKES 6 SERVINGS

MUSSELS TO STEW

At the beginning of a big shore dinner, it's traditional to start out with a large number of mollusks—either clams or oysters on the half shell, or mussels or steamers in their juices.

Mussels

Water

Mace

Butter

Flour

Bread

Wash the mussels two or three times to clean off all the sand. Then put them into a covered stew pan filled with water and let them stew until all the shells are opened and pick them out of their shells. When they are all picked, and any crabs are discarded, put them into a saucepan over medium heat. For every quart of mussels put half a pint of the strained (through a hair sieve) liquor that came from the stewing. Add a blade of mace and a walnut-sized piece of butter rolled in flour. Let the mussels simmer, and when done sufficiently, toast some triangular slices of bread and lay them around a dish. Pour in the mussels and serve hot.

GOURMET CHILI

All Yankee chili contains beans. In Texas, that would be a culinary sin, but we like to think of this type of chili less as a variation of the kind they make in Texas and more as a curious kind of farmhouse chowder—a hearty one-dish preparation that will last for several meals. The "gourmet" aspect of it comes from the taste of wine. Needless to say, you're not going to be using Château Lafite Rothschild in the recipe. A barely drinkable burgundy will do just fine.

3	*pounds dry kidney beans*
3	*pounds hamburger*
6	*cloves garlic, chopped*
3	*large onions*
3	*tablespoons cumin*
6	*tablespoons chili powder*
3	*tablespoons Worcestershire sauce*
3	*(26-ounce) cans whole tomatoes, blended*
3	*green peppers*
3	*cups Burgundy wine*
	Salt and pepper

Boil the kidney beans for 2 to 3 minutes, and then soak them for 1 hour; drain. Sauté the hamburger, garlic, and onion. Put in a large pot with the beans. Add the cumin, chili powder, Worcestershire sauce, tomatoes, peppers, wine, and salt and pepper to taste. Simmer for at least 1 hour.

MAKES ABOUT 2 GALLONS

· SAUCES ·

HORSERADISH SAUCE

The most famous meal at Durgin-Park is prime rib, the mellow luxury of which is amplified by a small measure of fresh, hot horseradish sauce. Keep the sauce refrigerated once you make it, and serve it soon after it's made. Over time, it loses its bite.

8	*tablespoons grated horseradish root*
5	*tablespoons vinegar*
1½	*teaspoons salt*
	Few grains of cayenne

Mix together the horseradish, vinegar, salt, and cayenne and bring to a boil. Remove from the heat at once. Let stand for 10 minutes. Bottle in sterilized jars.

MAKES 1 CUP

LAURA THE WAITRESS

LAURA DOES NOT hesitate to complain about the tribulations of being a waitress at Durgin-Park, but it's clear that she was meant for the job. And even as she grumbles about everything that bothers her, it becomes apparent that she loves being part of the waitstaff. An energetic woman up to the task of carrying armloads of heavy-cut prime rib plates, she originally came to Durgin-Park because a friend, Richelle, was a waitress and recommended her. That's often the way it works in this close-knit place: friends recommend friends and relatives, and it's all in the family. Compared to most restaurants, there is little turnover of personnel in the kitchen or on the dining room floor. Once you come to Durgin-Park, you tend to stay.

"It's not easy working here," Laura says. "It's hot, it's stressful, and you have to put up with tourists. They ask a million questions, like 'How many beans are there in a bowl?' or 'Do you have a *dietetic* cut of prime rib?' Someone says that, I tell them to get the hell out. If you work here, you have to learn to take a lot of crap . . . and to give it back."

Laura is heir to a tradition of outspoken waitresses. One of the most famous, who only recently retired, was Dottie Lamb,

Angie and Dottie taking a break.

who started work at Durgin-Park in the early 1960s. Dottie, who late in her career was known to wear a button on her blouse that read *Beyond Bitch* (given to her by a customer she had abused), once told an interviewer from *Yankee* magazine, "People are so stupid! They ask me, 'What's the duck stuffed with?' Well, it's not stuffed with feathers. It's stuffed with stuffing." *Yankee* also quoted Dottie as being particularly irked by a customer she identified as being from the More family: "More butter, more bread, more silverware."

Waitresses of Drugin-Park Working the line.

One time when she got fed up with his demands, she dropped a hot potato in the man's lap. He was the one who gave her the Beyond Bitch lapel pin.

No current waitress would purposely drop food onto a customer; in fact, Laura considers the regulars who dine at Durgin-Park good friends. "They come in every day at lunch and sit at the singles table and order the same thing they always get," she says. "We have one guy who sits down and asks, 'What's fresh?' five days a week. And five days a week, I tell him, 'Everything.'"

Hard work at Durgin-Park can be fun.

Known for their sass, Durgin-Park waitresses have many loyal customers.

Laura says that the familial character of Durgin-Park is such that many customers have met their spouses at the communal tables, married here in the dining rooms, and return every year to celebrate their wedding anniversaries.

"I don't think I'll ever leave," she says. "Once you work at Durgin-Park, you never forget it . . . and you can never work anyplace else."

MINT JELLY

Lamb is a fairly rare dish on menus everywhere in the nation. Nearly every restaurant that serves it offers mint jelly on the side. Like everything else from Durgin-Park's kitchen, its version of mint jelly is labor intensive, truly made from scratch, made the old, old-fashioned way.

6	*pounds firm tart apples*
4	*cups water*
	Sugar
1	*large bunch mint leaves*

Wash, core, and slice the apples (do not peel). In a large saucepan combine the apples and the water and bring to a boil. Turn the temperature to low and cook for 15 minutes or until the apples are soft. Once soft, remove the apples from the heat and pour them through a jelly bag or large sieve lined with several layers of cheesecloth. Let the juice drip into a measuring bowl. (Do not squeeze the bag.) Add ¾ cup sugar for every cup of juice and pour back into the saucepan. Boil the liquid for 20 minutes and skim the surface. Before removing the jelly from the fire, bruise the leaves of a bunch of fresh mint and add. Add a small amount of green coloring. Remove the leaves when the desired strength of mint flavor is obtained. Pour into sterilized glass jars and seal. Put in a sunny window and let stand for 24 hours.

FILLS 8 (8-OUNCE) JARS

RAISIN SAUCE FOR BAKED HAM

This sauce is an alternative to the sauce on the next page.

2	*cups orange juice*
1	*cup pineapple juice*
¼	*cup light brown sugar*
¼	*cup raisins*
¼	*cup soy sauce*
	Cornstarch

Place the orange juice, pineapple juice, brown sugar, raisins, and soy sauce in a small saucepan and bring to a boil. Simmer for 4 to 5 minutes. To thicken the mixture, combine equal parts cornstarch and water and add to the sauce.

MAKES ABOUT 2 CUPS

RAISIN SAUCE FOR HAM

Serve this raisin sauce hot, either as a gravy for a whole ham about to be served (spooning up some to blanket every plateful) or in a pitcher so everyone at the table can ladle it out as needed.

1	*cup seedless raisins*
1	*cup sugar*
¼	*cup cider vinegar*
½	*teaspoon salt*
⅛	*teaspoon cloves*
1	*(8-ounce jar) currant or grape jelly*

Soak the raisins in lukewarm water until plumped. Pour off the water. Add the sugar, vinegar, salt, cloves, and jelly. Heat before serving. Good with hot or cold ham.

MAKES ABOUT 3 CUPS

MARINARA SAUCE

Boston is one of America's great Italian-food cities. Combine that with its bounty of North Atlantic seafood and you've got the makings of an Italian-American feast.

½	cup olive oil
1	cup minced onion
4	cloves fresh garlic, minced
1	pound beef flank steak, or your choice
1	pound pork bones, with meat
1	pound veal bones, with meat
1	pound lamb shank, cut into 2-inch pieces
1	(6-pound, 10-ounce) can crushed tomatoes
4	cups water
2	tablespoons salt
2	bay leaves
1	teaspoon crushed red pepper
2	tablespoons oregano
2	tablespoons basil
1	teaspoon thyme
2	(6-ounce) cans tomato paste

Using a large heavy saucepan with a tight-fitting cover, heat the olive oil. Sauté the onion and garlic until lightly browned. Add the meats, and sauté, turning occasionally. Add the tomatoes, water, salt, bay leaves, red pepper, oregano, basil, and thyme. Stir until well combined. Cover the pot, and simmer for 6 hours. Uncover. Add the tomato paste, stirring to blend; simmer uncovered for 2 hours, or until the sauce is thickened. Stir occasionally. Remove the bones and bay leaves and discard.

MAKES 10 SERVINGS

TARTAR SAUCE

When you serve cooked fish in large portions, no matter how delicious, it is spritzed with fresh lemon juice, there comes a point in the meal when taste buds grow blasé to its flavor. That is when some tartar sauce can step in and rejuvenate the palate. Of course, those who love tartar sauce apply it to each and every bite of schrod or salmon or any fish that's fried. And if there's some left over, you can use it as a dip for bread.

---

2   *cups salad dressing-type mayonnaise*
1   *cup dill pickle relish*
1   *small onion, finely chopped*

Mix together the mayonnaise, pickle relish, and onion. Chill.

MAKES ABOUT 3½ CUPS

CONDIMENTS

CONDIMENTS ARE among the many traditions at Durgin-Park that never change. "When I arrived forty years ago, it was the same things on the table as we have now," chef Tommy Ryan says with a measure of pride. "Lea & Perrins [Worcestershire sauce], A-1, Gulden's mustard, Tabasco sauce, and Heinz ketchup." Tommy's deep-set belief in the array of familiar store-shelf bottles reflects an attitude that is common among old-time cooks, especially in New England: a firm belief in top-shelf brands. "All name-brands, all the best," he boasts, the implication being that lesser restaurants and less exacting cooks would offer no-name condiments of inferior quality. That's the paradox of Durgin-Park cuisine. While thrifty in character, it is never stingy in its larder. Quality goods are essential to the way this kitchen cooks. Culinary frills are anathema, but excellent ingredients are obligatory.

Condiments are particularly important in this regard because Yankee cooking is so straightforward. The philosophy here is that food should taste like what it is, without kaleidoscopes of spice and rivers of sauce. For many eaters, one of the pleasures of eating such plain food is the opportunity to exactly season it to taste, using such adornments as A-1 and Tabasco sauce.

In addition to what's on the table, one more condiment is available by request: horseradish. "That, we keep in the refrigerator," Tommy explains. "You have to ask for it. Our roast beef eaters know that."

• SIDE DISHES •

BOSTON BAKED BEANS

If you want to see someone get riled, go to chef Tommy Ryan and mention the food company that came out a while ago with a product called Boston Style Baked Beans. "Boston style!" he scoffs. "They had tomatoes and all kinds of spices in there. I say it might have been some kind of chili, but it was not beans, not baked beans as we know them." He points out that baked beans containing no tomatoes have been named the official state bean by the legislature, not to mention the fact that Boston's semiofficial nickname is Beantown, meaning Boston's own Durgin-Park ought to know how to make them. Although beans baked with salt pork are no longer considered the regular Saturday night supper in local homes, one out of five Durgin-Park customers orders them, and it would be inconceivable to have a plate of fish cakes without them. "The sweetness of the beans is a nice complement to the fish cakes, which we make good and salty," Tommy says.

1	pound (2 cups) dried navy beans
½	pound salt pork, cut in half
½	cup sugar
⅔	cup dark molasses
1	teaspoon dry mustard
1	teaspoon white pepper
1	teaspoon salt

Soak the beans overnight in cold water. The beans will double in size. Place the beans in a heavy saucepan, fill with water half an inch above the beans, and boil for 25 to 30 minutes. The beans will be tender; do not overcook. (Place a bean between thumb and forefinger and pinch. The outer shell should slip off.) Drain and rinse, saving the stock. Preheat the oven to 400°F. Place half the salt pork in the bottom of a large ovenproof pot. Add the beans, sugar, molasses, dry mustard, white pepper, and salt. Top with the remaining half of the salt pork. Bake for 4 to 4½ hours. Let the beans rest for 30 minutes before serving.

MAKES 6 TO 8 SERVINGS

HERBED RICE

Broiled schrod is one of the signature dishes of the Durgin-Park kitchen. It is a supremely mild fillet of fish, pure white and subtle. This flavorful rice makes a nice complement to schrod or any other gentle-flavored fish or chicken.

½	cup diced celery
½	cup diced onion
½	cup diced carrots
¼	cup oil
1½	cups uncooked rice
1	bay leaf
1	teaspoon dried thyme
½	teaspoon dried dill
3	cups chicken stock
2	teaspoons salt
½	teaspoon pepper

In a large, ovenproof skillet, sauté the celery, onion, and carrots in the oil until soft. Add the rice, bay leaf, thyme, and dill and stir to coat the rice with the oil. Heat the chicken stock and add to the rice with the salt and pepper. Preheat the oven to 350°F. Bring the rice to a boil and bake for 30 to 45 minutes or until all the liquid is absorbed.

MAKES 6 TO 8 SERVINGS

MACARONI AND CHEESE

In Colonial days, the word *macaroni* referred not to noodles but to anything that was ultra-fancy (which is why Yankee Doodle "stuck a feather in his hat and called it macaroni"). Long before noodles were known as pasta, macaroni and cheese became a comfort-food staple of the American diet, especially popular in the Northeast. A close relative of old-fashioned Welsh rarebit, this is a nice side dish for almost any main course meat. Add a few pieces of bacon and it's a meal.

---

2   *cups elbow macaroni*

4   *tablespoons butter*

4   *tablespoons flour*

3   *cups milk*

6   *ounces grated sharp Cheddar cheese*

Heat the oven to 350°F. Butter a 2-quart casserole. Bring a large pan of water to a boil. Add the macaroni and cook for 7 minutes, stirring once or twice. Drain the macaroni in a colander. In a saucepan, melt the butter and stir in the flour. Cook for 2 minutes, stirring constantly. Slowly add the milk and continue cooking and stirring over medium heat until the mixture thickens. Remove the sauce from the heat, and mix in the cheese until it melts and the sauce is smooth. Toss the macaroni and sauce together in the casserole. Bake for 30 minutes or until golden on top. Do not overbake. Serve at once.

MAKES 6 SERVINGS

MASHED POTATOES WITH CHÈVRE

The chèvre adds a creamy/tangy *je ne sais quois* to the standard mashed potato recipe. Of course, it is also possible to make them without *je ne sais quois,* by substituting plenty of butter for the goat cheese. That's the traditional way at Durgin-Park, where the already-buttery mashed potatoes are served with extra pats of butter on the side for melting atop the creamy white pile.

Mashed potatoes, to be good, must be made from scratch. At Durgin-Park, large all-purpose potatoes from Maine or Canada are thrown into a potato peeler machine that looks like a giant washing machine. When they come out, they are inspected, one-by-one, and hand-trimmed of any "eyes" and left-on skin. They are then boiled and whipped with milk or half-and-half and butter. *Warm* milk or half-and-half, Tommy Ryan reminds us. If it's cold, you may wind up with gluey potatoes.

3	*pounds potatoes, peeled and quartered*
¼	*cup (½ stick) butter, at room temperature*
7	*ounces fresh soft chèvre, cut into thick slices, at room temperature*
⅔	*cup half-and-half*
	Salt and white pepper
	Ground nutmeg for garnish (optional)

In a large saucepan cover the potatoes with cold water; cover the pan, and bring the potatoes to a boil. Lower the heat to medium and cook for 25 to 30 minutes or until the potatoes are fork-tender. Drain. Heat the butter, chèvre, and half-and-half until the cheese melts. Add the butter mixture to the drained potatoes and mash them until they are smooth, adding more warmed half-and-half if a thinner mixture is desired. Season with the salt and pepper to taste, transfer to a serving bowl, and sprinkle nutmeg, if using, lightly over the top of the potatoes.

MAKES 8 TO 10 SERVINGS

The restaurant that indisputably boasts "Established Before You Were Born" came into existence a few decades before the Boston Tea Party as a place where the men who sold meat and produce in the city's Faneuil Hall Marketplace could have a place to sit down and have their morning meal.

Although Durgin-Park is a restaurant of no frills as the red checkered table-cloths indicate, there is a more elegant dining room for private parties on the third floor with white tablecloths.

Behind the scenes special care is taken by everyone in the kitchen to produce the freshest food from the hours old fish to the fresh baked corn bread.

Although they don't put up with any nonsense, Durgin-Park's outspoken waitresses are friendly and efficient.

Head Chef Tommy Ryan insists on the Durgin-Park way, which includes thriftiness. This is exhibited in the steamers (right) that run on steam from the restaurants boiler and the dumbwaiter (below) that uses the same mechanical pulley system of a hundred years ago

Another aspect of the Durgin-Park way is the care taken in preparation. Tommy has all the apples (left) and carrots (below) peeled by hand.

Durgin-Park is a restaurant of tradition that has lasted for over 100 years. Part of that tradition are the Boston baked beans (right) that are hand cooked in the famous Durgin-Park bean pots (below).

MASHED TURNIPS

Shopping tip: The younger the turnips, the smoother their texture. Few dishes are more typically Yankee than mashed turnips, which are the standard companion to turkey, stuffing, and mashed potatoes, especially on a holiday table.

6	*pounds turnips, peeled*
½	*cup (1 stick) butter, melted*
2	*tablespoons salt*
2	*tablespoons pepper*
¼	*teaspoon ground nutmeg*

Preheat the oven to 325°F. Toss the turnips and the butter in a 13 x 9 x 2-inch glass baking dish. Sprinkle the turnips with salt and pepper. Cover the dish with foil. Bake until tender, about 1 hour. Remove from the oven and coarsely mash the turnips. Stir in the nutmeg before serving.

MAKES 12 SERVINGS

ONION CASSEROLE

Durgin-Park is known as a place to eat meat . . . or at least big slabs of fish or whole lobsters. Its side dishes get little of the glory, but their abundance and goodness are a vital part of the Durgin-Park experience. In fact, while few people think of it this way, it is a great place to have an all-vegetable meal. One of the most substantial vegetable recipes we know is this onion casserole from Tommy Ryan's kitchen. With something green on the side, it's a veritable meal.

2	*large Vidalia onions, chopped*
2	*tablespoons butter plus 2 tablespoons melted butter*
1	*(10¾-ounce) can undiluted cream of chicken soup*
½	*cup milk*
1	*teaspoon soy sauce*
2	*cups shredded Swiss cheese*
½	*loaf French bread*

Preheat the oven to 350°F. Sauté the onions in 2 tablespoons butter until tender. Spoon the onions into an 8-inch casserole. Combine the soup, milk, and soy sauce; pour over the onions. Sprinkle the cheese on top of the onions. Cut the bread into ¾-inch slices. Arrange the bread slices on top of the casserole and brush with the melted butter. Bake for 30 minutes.

MAKES 4 TO 6 SERVINGS

PARMESAN POTATO ROUNDS

A great companion for meat, fish, or fowl or as part of a "Bale of Hay" (Durgin-Park's all-vegetable meal), these potato rounds are just fine if you make them with the kind of Parmesan cheese that comes in a can. If you grate your own, they're magic.

4	*medium red potatoes, thinly sliced*
1	*small onion, thinly sliced and separated into rings*
3	*tablespoons butter or margarine, melted*
¼	*cup grated Parmesan cheese*
¼	*teaspoon salt*
⅛	*teaspoon pepper*
⅛	*teaspoon garlic powder*

Preheat the oven to 450°F. Place half the potatoes in a greased 1-quart or 11 x 7 x 2-inch baking dish. Top with the onion and remaining potatoes. Drizzle with the butter. Sprinkle with the Parmesan cheese, salt, pepper, and garlic powder. Bake uncovered for 25 to 30 minutes or until the potatoes are golden brown and tender.

MAKES 4 SERVINGS

RAW CABBAGE

When the Pilgrims arrived at Plymouth Rock, they carried cabbage seeds with them. The earliest recorded meals included this vegetable in its boiled form, then later as sauerkraut and, uncooked, as coleslaw. Durgin-Park's recipe for raw cabbage serves the same refreshing role as coleslaw on a plate of broiled fish.

4	cups chopped cabbage
½	cup sweet cream
2	tablespoons vinegar or lemon juice
1	cup sugar

In a large bowl mix together the chopped cabbage, sweet cream, vinegar or lemon juice, and sugar. Cover and refrigerate 1 hour before serving.

MAKES 4 TO 6 SERVINGS

SCALLOPED TOMATOES

While Durgin-Park abjures tomatoes in Boston baked beans, a serving of scalloped tomatoes makes a great third side dish for a hearty plate of meat, potatoes, and beans.

¼	cup butter
½	cup chopped green pepper
½	cup chopped onion
2	cups bread crumbs
⅓	cup Romano cheese plus extra for topping
¾	teaspoon salt
⅛	teaspoon pepper
4	medium tomatoes, peeled and sliced
	Chopped parsley

Preheat the oven to 350°F. In a medium saucepan melt the butter. Sauté the pepper and onion until tender, about 5 minutes. Remove from the heat. Stir in the bread crumbs, the ⅓ cup cheese, salt, and pepper. Arrange one-third of the tomatoes on a greased 10 x 6-inch casserole. Sprinkle with half the bread crumb mixture. Repeat the layers, using another one-third of the tomatoes and the remaining one-half of the crumb mixture. Top with the remaining one-third of the tomatoes. Bake for 45 minutes, or until the tomatoes are tender. When finished sprinkle the dish with the extra cheese and the parsley.

MAKES 4 TO 6 SERVINGS

SMOTHERED ONIONS

There isn't a recipe more basic than this one, which leaves it to the cook to determine the character of the onions. Lots of butter, a big Vidalia, and medium heat for a moderate amount of time will yield soft, caramel-sweet onions suitable for smothering just about any cut of beef. Use a sharper onion in a deep pool of butter over higher heat, and you can create crisp, dark squiggles with texture on the verge of crunch: great for topping any vegetable or casserole.

---

1   *large onion*
2   *tablespoons butter*
     Dash of white pepper

Slice the onion ⅛-inch thick. In a saucepan heat the butter over medium-high heat. Add the onion and white pepper and sauté for 5 minutes or until the onion is translucent. These can be eaten as a side dish or served over any steak or beef dish.

MAKES 2 TO 4 SERVINGS

STEWED TOMATOES

This is a very old-fashioned, luxurious kind of dish, evocative of the days, very long ago, when tomatoes were known among New Englanders as *love apples* and thought to be simply too sensuous to even think of eating.

2	*pounds vine-ripe tomatoes*
4	*tablespoons butter*
	Salt and pepper
1	*teaspoon sugar*

Remove the skins and pits of the tomatoes. Place them in a porcelain stew pan and cover with water. Boil briskly, partially covered, for 20 minutes. Then simmer slowly until the tomatoes are creamy, at least two hours. Season with butter, salt and pepper to taste, and sugar. Watch the heat since tomatoes burn suddenly.

MAKES 4 SERVINGS

STUFFED SQUASH

Acorn and butternut squashes are available in markets year-round, but their look, smell, and flavor are especially suited for autumn meals. It is also possible to bake the squash halves plain; then, while they're still hot, remove all the pulp from the skin and mix it with the apple-nut-maple stuffing.

1	*acorn or butternut squash*
¼	*cup plus 2 tablespoons melted butter*
1	*cup diced apple*
¼	*cup chopped nuts*
2	*tablespoons maple syrup*

Preheat the oven to 400°F. Cut the squash in half. Remove the seeds and brush the halves with the ¼ cup melted butter. In a bowl mix the apple, nuts, syrup, and 2 tablespoons melted butter. Fill the squash halves with the apple-nut mixture. Cover the squash with foil and bake for 45 to 60 minutes.

MAKES 2 SERVINGS

SUCCOTASH

The very basic combination of beans and corn with a bit of pork flavoring is a mighty fine accompaniment for beef or meat loaf . . . with potatoes and cornbread on the side, of course.

12	slices bacon
1	cup chopped onion
2	garlic cloves, minced
4	ears corn, kernels cut off the cobs
1	large fresh jalapeño chile, seeded and finely chopped
1	(10-ounce) package frozen baby lima beans, thawed
2½	cups sliced okra
2	cups halved cherry tomatoes
2	tablespoons cider vinegar
2	tablespoons dried basil
	Salt and pepper

Cook the bacon in a large skillet over medium heat until crisp. Drain the bacon on paper towels, leaving the fat in the skillet. Add the onion to the skillet and cook, stirring, until softened. Add the garlic and cook for 1 minute. Stir in the corn, jalapeño, lima beans, okra, and tomatoes; cook, stirring, until the vegetables are tender, about 7 minutes. Stir in the vinegar, basil, and salt and pepper to taste. Serve with the bacon crumbled over the top.

MAKES 8 SERVINGS

THE FREEDOM TRAIL

DURGIN-PARK ISN'T an official stop on the 2.5-mile walking tour around Boston known as the Freedom Trail, but it's a fundamental part of the scenery.

One of America's first historic walking tours, the Freedom Trail is an eye-opening journey that winds among sixteen sites that tell the story of how the United States began. Depending on how deeply you want to immerse yourself in the sites, you can do it in three hours or take a whole, leisurely day.

The tour begins at the Boston Common (America's oldest public park), then moves on to the State House, Park Street Church, Granary Burying Ground, King's Chapel, America's first public school (Boston Latin School, 1635), the Old Corner Book Store, Old South Meeting House (where the Boston Tea Party was initiated), Old State House, site of the Boston Massacre, Faneuil Hall, Paul Revere's House, Old North Church, Copp's Hill Burying Ground, the USS *Constitution*, and Bunker Hill Museum.

Faneuil Hall, which is known as the Cradle of Liberty because it was where Boston patriots vehemently protested British taxation policies, is about midway through the trip. And Durgin-Park is in its shadow. That means that if you start the tour mid-morning, Durgin-Park will be an ideal place to stop and have a lunch that is suitably historic.

For information about the Freedom Trail, visit www.thefreedomtrail.org.

TWICE BAKED POTATOES

New England food authority Brooke Dojny reports that potatoes were first planted in Boston by Irish immigrants in 1718, but they did not become widely popular until the nineteenth century. Victorian-era restaurant menus, including those from Durgin-Park, abound with potato dishes; it was not unusual a hundred years ago for a good restaurant to offer up to a dozen different kinds of potato, from baked to scalloped to Duchesse.

We have found that the best way to prepare potatoes suitable for twice-baking is to make that first bake long and slow—maybe 90 minutes at 375 degrees—so that the skin gets rugged and leathery and the inside is cream-soft.

4	*large baking potatoes*
½	*cup butter*
¼	*cup milk*
¼	*cup sour cream*
2	*tablespoons Parmesan cheese*
1½	*teaspoons salt*
½	*teaspoon onion powder*
	Dash of cayenne
	Paprika

Preheat the oven to 400°F. Wash the potatoes and bake until easily pierced with a fork, about 40 minutes. While still hot, carefully cut the potatoes in half lengthwise. Carefully remove the potatoes from the skins, leaving an ⅛-inch wall. Place the potato meat in a mixing bowl. Add the butter and milk, whipping until fluffy. Add the sour cream, Parmesan cheese, salt, onion powder, and cayenne. Beat well, adding more milk if necessary. Spoon the potato mixture back into the shells. Sprinkle lightly with the paprika. Place in a greased shallow baking dish. Reduce the oven temperature to 375°F and bake for 45 to 50 minutes.

MAKES 4 SERVINGS

ZUCCHINI PIE

Zucchini, God bless it, grows very, very well—so well that by midsummer virtually everyone with a garden has more than enough to keep and give away. As a result, creative cooks have invented countless good things to do with the indomitable vegetable. This jiffy pie is a savory vegetarian meal.

1	(8-ounce) can crescent rolls
2	teaspoons mustard
4	cups zucchini, thinly sliced
1	cup chopped onion
⅔	cup margarine
½	cup chopped parsley
½	teaspoon salt
½	teaspoon ground pepper
¼	teaspoon garlic powder
½	teaspoon basil
½	teaspoon oregano
2	beaten eggs
2	cups shredded mozzarella cheese

Preheat the oven to 375°F. Unroll the crescent rolls and press them into an ungreased, 10-inch pie plate. Spread with the mustard. Combine and steam briefly the zucchini, onion, margarine, parsley, salt, pepper, garlic powder, basil, and oregano. Combine the eggs and cheese and stir in the zucchini mixture. Pour into the crust. Cook for 18 to 20 minutes, covering the crust for the last 10 minutes of cooking time. Let stand for 10 minutes before serving.

MAKES 6 TO 8 SERVINGS

MAIN DISHES

BAKED FINNAN HADDIE

New York Times food critic Craig Claiborne once said, "You may tell the butler to dispense with the caviar, truffles, and nightingales' tongues." In the place of such exotica, what he preferred was "a platter of choice finnan haddie, freshly cooked in its bath of water and milk and melted butter, a slice or two of hot toast, and a pot of steaming Darjeeling tea."

2	pounds split, smoked haddock (not individual pieces)
1	cup whole milk
4	tablespoons butter
½	teaspoon pepper

Cut the haddock into individual servings. Place skin side down in a shallow buttered baking dish and add enough milk to partially cover the fish. Dot with butter. Sprinkle with pepper. Broil the fish in a preheated broiler until tender, about 20 minutes. Baste with the hot milk before serving. The milk remaining in the pan makes a delicious bouillon.

MAKES 4 SERVINGS

BAKED SEAFOOD WITH STUFFING

Stuffing—known in other parts of the country as dressing—can be served underneath, on top of, or adjacent to any nice portion of broiled seafood. It obviates the need for rice or potatoes and adds spice plus the intoxicating wisp of wine to otherwise simple-flavored foods.

Stuffing:

3	cups round buttery crackers, finely crushed
¾	cup plus 2 ounces melted butter
¼	cup sweet vermouth or sherry
¼	cup minced garlic
6	teaspoons white pepper
6	teaspoons Spanish paprika
6	dashes Worcestershire sauce
3	pounds fish of your choice

To make the stuffing, in a large bowl combine the crackers, butter, vermouth, garlic, pepper, paprika, and Worcestershire. Mix thoroughly and let sit for 10 minutes before fluffing with a fork. Preheat the oven to 350°F. Place the fish, scallops, or shrimp in a small casserole dish. Cover with the stuffing. Top with 2 ounces melted butter. Bake for 10 to 14 minutes.

MAKES 8 SERVINGS

BAKED STUFFED LOBSTER

Baked stuffed lobster is frequently the most expensive item on menus in the Northeast. While lobster purists want no part of any recipe that does anything to the king of the sea other than cook it, palates in search of extra luxury like to add a sumptuous dressing that counterpoints the lobster with the taste of other mollusks.

2	*(1-pound) lobsters*
2	*cups soft bread cubes*
4	*tablespoons melted butter*
1	*tablespoon grated onion*

If the lobsters have not been split at market, place the lobster on its back on a cutting board. With a sharp knife, split the lobster down the middle. Remove the membranes and vein from the tail. Preheat the oven to 400°F. Remove and save the green liver and coral roe. Combine the bread cubes, butter, onion, liver, and roe. Place mixture in the body cavity and over the surface of the tail meat. Bake for about 20 minutes, or until the stuffing is lightly browned.

MAKES 2 SERVINGS

BROILED LIVE LOBSTER

Steaming or boiling lobsters is fundamental, but broiling or grilling adds an indescribable succulence to the tender pink meat. Be generous when brushing the lobster with butter (and continue to brush it as it grills, lest it dry out). And do not overcook!

Lobster
Melted butter
Salt and pepper

If possible, have the lobsters split at the market. Otherwise hold the large claws firmly. With a sharp pointed knife, begin at the mouth and make an incision; split the shell the entire length of the body and tail. Remove the stomach and intestinal canal and a small sac just behind the head. Crack the large claws and lay the lobster as flat as possible. Brush the meat with melted butter. Season with salt and pepper to taste. Place in a broiler, shell side down. Broil slowly until a delicate brown, about 20 minutes. Serve hot with melted butter.

SERVE ½ LARGE OR 1 SMALL LOBSTER PER PERSON

BROILED SCHROD

Although schrod is one of the premier items on the seafood menu of Durgin-Park and many other regional restaurants where seafood is important, the fact is that there is no such fish. Schrod (pronounced *skrod*) is simply the name for young codfish. It is ineffably tender, pure white, and gently sweet.

1½   *pounds Codfish*
      Salt and pepper
2   *tablespoons melted butter*
¼   *cup bread crumbs*
2   *tablespoons lemon juice*

Select a young, fresh codfish and scrape to remove the scales, being careful not to break the skin. Cut into fillets without removing the skin. Season lightly to taste with salt and pepper, and then sprinkle with melted butter. Dip in fresh bread crumbs; sprinkle again with a little more melted butter. Broil each side for 10 to 15 minutes. Start the broiling with the flesh side down; when broiling with the skin side down, use care not to let the skin break. Serve very hot with a bowl of melted butter with a little lemon juice stirred in.

MAKES 5 SERVINGS

CRABMEAT AU GRATIN

This is a flexible recipe that makes not only a main course, but also hors d'oeuvres when portioned out by the tablespoonful.

2	tablespoons butter
1½	tablespoons flour
	Pinch of salt
⅛	teaspoon dry mustard
1	cup milk
½	teaspoon Worcestershire sauce
¼	pound Cheddar cheese, grated
4	cups crabmeat
¼	cup grated Parmesan cheese

Preheat the oven to 300°F. In a saucepan combine the butter, flour, salt, mustard, milk, and Worcestershire sauce. Stir over low heat until the butter melts and the mixture is blended. Stir in the Cheddar cheese and crabmeat. Place the mixture in a 2-quart baking dish or 6 scallop shells. Sprinkle the Parmesan cheese on top. Bake for 10 minutes or until piping hot.

MAKES 4 TO 6 SERVINGS

FILLETS OF SOLE COOKED IN CREAM

Years ago, every diligent young cook had a recipe for "wiggle" in her repertoire. Why it was called that, we don't know, but wiggle generally referred to the fine art of taking some kind of basic fish and lavishing it with lots of cream and butter. This Durgin-Park recipe makes simple sole into the soul of opulence.

6	*fillets of sole or flounder*
1	*cup cider*
1	*cup water*
1	*tablespoon lemon juice*
3	*plus 1½ tablespoons butter*
1	*teaspoon salt*
1	*teaspoon pepper*
1½	*tablespoons flour*
1	*cup heavy cream, sweet or sour*
2	*tablespoons finely grated Cheddar cheese*
2	*tablespoons finely chopped parsley*

Simmer the fillets in the cider, water, and lemon juice. Add the 3 tablespoons butter, salt, and pepper and cook for 10 minutes. Drain, reserving the liquid, and put the fish in a buttered, 2-quart baking dish. Preheat the oven to 350°F. Melt the remaining 1½ tablespoons butter in a saucepan and add the flour. Mix and simmer together for 3 minutes. Add the reserved liquid and cook for 5 more minutes; then add the heavy cream. Pour this sauce over the sole and bake until well browned, approximately 20 minutes. Garnish with grated cheese and parsley mixed together.

MAKES 4 SERVINGS

FISH CAKES

Fish cakes with baked beans is an immemorial Boston recipe, and Durgin-Park is one of the handful of local restaurants that continue to serve it, every day. As chef Tommy Ryan emphasized the vital importance of making mashed potatoes from scratch, he shared the fact that it's always a good thing to make extra mashed potatoes . . . because you'll need them to make your fish cakes.

2	*pounds fresh cod*
2	*pounds fresh pollock*
6	*to 8 celery ribs, minced*
1	*large onion, minced*
6	*teaspoons kosher salt*
6	*teaspoons white pepper*
6	*dashes Worcestershire sauce*
1	*cup mashed potatoes*
½	*cup bread crumbs*
¼	*pound (1 stick) butter*

Preheat the oven to 375°F. In a large casserole dish, cook the fish with the onion and celery; add the salt, pepper, and Worcestershire sauce. Cook for about 10 minutes or until the fish falls apart. Drain the fish and place in a mixing bowl. Add the potatoes and the bread crumbs and mix. Make two 3-ounce fish cakes; coat the cakes with the bread crumbs and either fry or broil them until browned, about 7 to 10 minutes.

MAKES 2 FISH CAKES

FLUFFY FISH CAKES

This is an alternative recipe for fish cakes for those times when you don't have any leftover mashed potatoes. If made small enough, these fish cakes also serve as a good hors d'oeuvre, served with tartar sauce or cocktail sauce (or both).

1½	*cups shredded codfish*
4	*medium-sized potatoes*
1	*egg, beaten*
½	*teaspoon pepper*
⅓	*cup light cream*
	Crushed cornflakes

Freshen the codfish by separating the pieces. Peel and dice the potatoes. Place the fish and potatoes in a pot of water and boil until the potatoes are soft. Drain. Add the egg, pepper, and cream; beat until fluffy. Form into balls or cakes, roll in finely crushed corn-flakes, and pan-fry or fry in hot deep fat until golden brown.

MAKES 4 SERVINGS

FRESH HALIBUT ON TOAST

Open-face sandwiches such as these are a way of making an otherwise lean fish such as halibut into something lush and luxy. Cosseted in cream sauce, halibut is here a gentle-mannered midday meal suitable for family and company.

2	pounds halibut
2	tablespoons butter
2	tablespoons flour
1	cup milk, heated
1	cup light cream
8	rounds toast, buttered
1	hard-boiled egg, chopped
	Salt and pepper

In a saucepan cover the fish with cold water and bring to a boil slowly. Drain the fish in a colander and flake apart with a fork. In the saucepan blend the butter and flour, and simmer for 1 minute over medium heat. Add the heated milk slowly. Add the cream and stir. When the sauce is smooth, add the fish. Cook until thickened. Serve on the toast. Garnish with the chopped egg. Season with the salt and pepper to taste.

MAKES 4 SERVINGS

GRILLED SALMON

A nearly forgotten tradition of New England is the Independence Day salmon supper: fresh fillets, grilled outdoors over a charcoal fire, are served with tender new potatoes and peas. For dessert: ice cream, of course!

⅓	*cup butter*
⅔	*cup dark brown sugar*
2	*tablespoons lemon juice*
2	*tablespoons minced, fresh tarragon*
	Salt and pepper
8	*(10- to 12-ounce) salmon fillets*

In a medium saucepan melt the butter over low heat. Add the brown sugar and stir until dissolved. Add the lemon juice, tarragon, and salt and pepper to taste, stirring until heated thoroughly, about 3 minutes. Place the fillets in a well-greased grill basket and brush with the sauce. Grill directly over medium coals for 4 to 6 minutes per ½ inch thickness. Turn once during cooking. Brush the salmon occasionally with the basting sauce during cooking and again just before serving.

MAKES 8 SERVINGS

THE THIRD MONDAY IN APRIL

To many Bostonians, Patriots' Day is right up there in significance with Independence Day. Formally recognized only in Maine and Massachusetts, Patriots' Day commemorates The Shot Heard Round the World and the skirmish that took place on April 19, 1775, between Minutemen and British Redcoats.

Despite its unquestioned historical significance, Patriots' Day is a regional holiday little-known outside the Northeast, and today the third Monday in April is better known to many Americans as Marathon Monday, the day of the legendary Boston Marathon.

The Marathon itself is a longstanding event, getting its inspiration from the Olympic Marathon of 1896, after which team manager John Graham decided to inaugurate a similar event in Boston. The original Boston Marathon of 1897 was 24.5 miles, based on the length of the run of Greek foot-soldier Pheidippides, who is said to have gone from the plains of Marathon to Athens with the news of victory over the Persian army. Boston's first Marathon went from the city's Irvington Oval to Metcalf's Mill in Ashland. That race featured fifteen competitors. The winner, John McDermott of New York, won it in 2:55:10.

From 1897 through 1968, the Boston Marathon was always held on Patriots' Day, unless the nineteenth happened to fall on a Sunday, in which case the race was rescheduled for Monday. Starting in 1969, Patriots' Day in Massachusetts was officially moved to the third Monday in April, and so was the Marathon.

Durgin-Park did not yet exist as an eating place when the Minutemen fought the British, but it stands in the shadow of Faneuil Hall, the meeting place where Samuel Adams and other Boston patriots spoke out against tyranny and fanned the flames of revolution.

LEMON HERBED SALMON

When it's too cold to cook salmon outside or when you are looking for a preparation that is more deluxe than simple grilling, this large herbed salmon fillet makes a great impression. It has such flavor and character all its own that we like to serve it with plain potatoes or white rice and a green vegetable with no adornment other than butter, salt, and pepper.

2½	cups fresh bread crumbs
4	garlic cloves, minced
½	cup chopped parsley
6	tablespoons grated Parmesan cheese
¼	cup chopped fresh thyme, or 1 tablespoon dried thyme
2	teaspoons grated lemon peel
½	teaspoon salt
4	plus 2 tablespoons butter or margarine, melted
1	(3- to 4-pound) salmon fillet

Preheat the oven to 350°F. In a bowl combine the bread crumbs, garlic, parsley, cheese, thyme, lemon peel, and salt; mix well. Add the 4 tablespoons of butter, and toss lightly. Pat the salmon dry. Place the salmon skin side down in a greased baking dish. Brush with the remaining 2 tablespoons butter; cover with the crumb mixture. Bake for 25 to 30 minutes.

MAKES 8 SERVINGS

LOBSTER NEWBURG

Creamy-rich Lobster Newburg was first served in New York at Delmonico's restaurant in 1876. It was named Lobster à la Wenberg for a customer named Ben Wenberg, who introduced the dish to Delmonico's chef. But Wenberg had a fight with the management (the details of which are sketchy), so he got dissed by the rechristening of the dish with his name in jumbled letters. When all this happened, Durgin-Park already was a well-established eatery, but Lobster Newburg did not appear on the menu until the mid-twentieth century.

6	tablespoons butter
2	tablespoons flour
3	cups lobster meat, cooked
	Dash of paprika
1	teaspoon salt
3	tablespoons sherry
3	egg yolks
2	cups cream

Melt the butter in the top of a double boiler over boiling water. Stir in the flour. Add the lobster then the paprika, salt, and sherry. Place over hot water. In a separate bowl slightly beat the egg yolks; add the cream and mix well. Stir slowly into the lobster. Cook slowly, stirring constantly until thickened.

MAKES 4 TO 5 SERVINGS

LOBSTER ROLLS

Oh, the joys of summer on the shoreline! In New England, those joys necessarily include a freshly made lobster roll, served in the split and grilled hot-dog bun that is so beloved in local seafood shacks (to hold heaps of fried clams, scallops, etc.), as well as wiener joints. There are basically two kinds of lobster roll: the lobster salad roll, as given in this recipe, and the hot lobster roll, which is nothing but buttered lobster meat in a grilled and buttered bun.

2	live (1¼ to 1⅓-pound) Maine lobsters
2	celery ribs, finely chopped
2	teaspoons finely chopped Vidalia or sweet Spanish onion
½	cup mayonnaise
	Salt and white pepper
	Butter, at room temperature
4	hot dog rolls

Bring a large pot of salted water to a boil. Plunge the lobsters into the pot, head first. Partially cover the pot and when the water returns to a boil, cover and boil for 10 minutes. Remove the lobsters with tongs and let them cool. Split the lobsters lengthwise and crack the claws. Remove the meat from the shells and cut into ½-inch pieces. Transfer to a large bowl. Add the celery, onion, mayonnaise, salt and pepper to taste and toss lightly. Preheat the broiler. Butter the rolls and place them on a shallow pan buttered side up. Broil the rolls about 6 inches from the heat until they are golden brown, about 3 minutes. Fill the rolls with the lobster salad and serve immediately.

MAKES 4 SERVINGS

OYSTER OR LOBSTER PIE

In most parts of the country, the name of this recipe would seem to be a misnomer. This is not a potpie with vegetables or a chicken pie with a crust; it is nothing but sweet ocean meat—oysters or lobster—cosseted in butter and cream. It would be a crime to gunk up a dish so pure and good with breadcrumbs or vegetables. Of course, the basis of its goodness is fresh oysters or lobster meat; and the key is not to overcook them.

2	tablespoons butter
9	select oysters, or 6 ounces fresh lobster meat
	Pinch of celery salt
	Pinch of white pepper
	Dash of Tabasco sauce
	Dash of Worcestershire sauce
	Pinch of kosher salt
1	cup heavy cream

Melt the butter in a sauté pan and add either the oysters or the lobster meat. If using the oysters, cook for 3 to 4 minutes or until the outside edges start to curl. If using the lobster meat, just warm in the butter. Add the celery salt, white pepper, Tabasco sauce, Worcestershire sauce, and kosher salt. Blend well. Add the heavy cream. Bring to a boil, but do not fully boil. Simmer for 5 to 6 minutes and serve.

MAKES 4 SERVINGS

SAUTÉED SCALLOPS

Scallops are always on the Durgin-Park menu—a handful as hors d'oeuvres, wrapped in bacon, or an abundance of them, sautéed in butter and served as a main course with potatoes and vegetables on the side.

1	cup flour
¼	teaspoon garlic powder
½	teaspoon paprika
1½	pounds scallops
¼	cup melted butter

In a bowl combine the flour, garlic powder, and paprika. Dredge the scallops in the flour mixture. Sauté in the butter for about 10 minutes or until brown.

MAKES 4 SERVINGS

SEAFOOD PIE

In the Midwest, they'd call this a hot dish, meaning it is the homey sort of casserole that few restaurants make but is a staple of family meals.

1	(6-ounce) package frozen crabmeat
1	(6-ounce) can tuna, drained
1	cup shredded, processed, sharp American cheese
3	ounces cream cheese, cut into ¼-inch slices
¼	cup green onions, sliced
2	ounces chopped pimiento, drained
2	cups milk
1	cup biscuit mix
4	eggs
¾	teaspoon salt
	Dash of nutmeg

Heat the oven to 400°F. Grease a deep dish pie plate. Mix the crabmeat, tuna, cheeses, onions, and pimiento in the pie plate. Beat the milk, biscuit mix, eggs, salt, and nutmeg until smooth (15 seconds in a blender or one minute with hand beater). Pour over the seafood mixture. Bake until a knife inserted between the center and the edge comes out clean, about 35 to 40 minutes. Cool for 5 minutes.

MAKES 4 TO 6 SERVINGS

SWORDFISH BOSTON STYLE

Boston-style" equals *basic* in this recipe, which depends entirely on a first-rate piece of fish. The tastiest swordfish anywhere are caught in the deep Atlantic waters southeast of Rhode Island Sound . . . which is one reason Boston is such a good place to eat them.

1	*(3-pound) slice swordfish*
4	*plus 4 tablespoons soft butter*
¾	*cup fine bread crumbs*
	Lemon wedges

Preheat the broiler. Coat one side of the fish with 4 tablespoons butter. Pat on half the bread crumbs. Broil 5 minutes; turn and repeat on the other side. More butter may be needed to prevent the fish from drying out. Serve with the lemon wedges.

MAKES 5 TO 6 SERVINGS

BAKED CHICKEN AND NOODLES

Been invited to a covered-dish dinner? Having a family reunion? When you want large portions of homey food without going to great expense, few meals satisfy as totally as a casserole of chicken and noodles. Little else is needed to make a meal of it—maybe a small salad to start, some ice cream for dessert.

1	(6-pound) stewing hen
2	large carrots, halved
2	celery ribs, halved
2	medium onions, quartered
8	black peppercorns
4	quarts water
1	plus 1 cup plus 3 tablespoons butter
1	pound fresh mushrooms, coarsely chopped
1	pound medium-wide noodles
3	hard-cooked eggs, coarsely chopped
½	cup chopped parsley
1	cup all-purpose flour
	Salt and white pepper
4	cups finely crushed round buttery crackers

Place the hen, including the neck and the giblets (but not the liver), in a large stockpot. Add the carrots, celery, onions, peppercorns, and water. (The water should liberally cover the chicken—you need lots of broth for this recipe.) Cover and bring to a boil over high heat, skimming off any froth that forms on top of the stock. Reduce the heat and simmer covered for 2 hours or until the chicken is very tender. Meanwhile, over medium-low heat, melt the 3 tablespoons butter in a large skillet. Add the mushrooms and sauté until golden brown, about 10 minutes. When the chicken is done, remove it from the broth with tongs, transfer it to a shallow pan, and allow it to cool a bit; then cut up the meat in fairly large pieces, discarding the bones and skin. Strain the broth and degrease. Remove 7 cups of the broth from the stockpot. Set aside. Bring the remaining broth to a boil, adding additional water if necessary, and add the noodles. Cook according to package directions until tender and drain.

Preheat the oven to 375°F. Grease two 3-quart, 9 x 13-inch, flat casseroles and in each dish, layer the noodles, chicken, mushrooms, eggs, and parsley, beginning and ending with the noodles. In a large saucepan melt 1 cup of the butter over medium-high heat. Whisk in the flour, cooking and stirring until it bubbles and becomes a smooth paste. Whisk in the reserved 7 cups of broth and continue cooking and stirring until the mixture thickens into a gravy, about 10 minutes. Add the salt and pepper to taste. Pour the gravy over the layers of chicken and noodles, making sure it gets down into the bottom of each dish. In a small saucepan melt the remaining 1 cup of butter and toss with the crushed crackers. Top each pan evenly with the crumbs. Bake the casseroles for 1 hour or until they are heated through and the crumbs are golden brown.

[Note: You may freeze this dish before baking, but do not top with the crumbs until you are ready to bake it.]

MAKES 16 TO 20 SERVINGS

CHICKEN LIVERS AND BACON

The secrets of delicious chicken livers are first, freshness—get them straight from the butcher—and second, a short cooking time. Sizzle them briefly at a high temperature, and they will be meltingly tender and perfectly partnered with slices of crisp bacon.

¼	cup shortening
1	pound chicken livers
½	cup butter
¼	cup dry vermouth or sherry
3	pieces bacon, cooked

Heat the shortening in a hot skillet and sear the chicken livers until they are brown all over. Remove the livers from the shortening. In a small sauté pan heat the butter and sauté the chicken livers for 5 to 8 minutes. During the last minute, add the vermouth. Serve with three pieces of cooked bacon, or Smothered Onions (page 88).

MAKES 2 TO 4 SERVINGS

CHICKEN POT PIE

One of the lesser-known facets of Yankee gastronomic history is the popularity of "farm wife pies." When much of the Northeast was still rural, it was common for country women to make pies (both sweet and savory) that they sold to neighbors and passers-by from their back porch off the kitchen.

1	*(5-pound) roasting chicken*
6	*medium carrots, diced*
1	*(16-ounce) can peas*
8	*ounces chicken stock*
6	*teaspoons celery salt*
6	*teaspoons white ground pepper*
4	*tablespoons butter*
4	*tablespoons plus 1 cup flour*
2	*teaspoons baking powder*
	Dash of salt
2	*eggs, beaten*
½	*cup milk*
1½	*teaspoons melted butter*

In a large pot cover the chicken with water and boil for one hour. Remove the chicken from the pot and let cool. Remove the skin and bones and cut the chicken into bite-sized pieces. Return the chicken to the stockpot. Add the carrots, peas, chicken base, celery salt, and white pepper. Drain the chicken stock into a separate pot. Heat the 4 tablespoons flour and 4 tablespoons butter in a pan to make a roux. Whisk it into the pot with the chicken stock to make the gravy to desired thickness. Turn the chicken mixture into a large casserole and cover with the gravy.

To make the crust, preheat the oven to 450°F. In a bowl stir together the 1 cup flour, baking powder, salt, eggs, milk, and melted butter until moist. Drop in small rounds on top of the hot gravy. Bake for 10 minutes. Reduce heat to 400°F, and cook 10 more minutes.

MAKES 12 SERVINGS

COUNTRY CHICKEN

Fowl has been an important part of the Yankee diet since the day the Pilgrims shot and cooked an eagle and declared it to be nearly as tasty as mutton. For those of us who prefer to procure our meat in a supermarket case, wrapped in plastic, this recipe for smothered chicken is much more practical. And it doesn't taste a bit like mutton!

¼	cup flour
1	teaspoon salt
1	teaspoon pepper
4	chicken breasts, boned and skinned
2	plus 4 tablespoons butter
¼	cup chopped green pepper
¼	cup chopped onion
¼	cup chopped celery
1	clove garlic, minced
½	cup sliced mushrooms
1	(15-ounce) can stewed tomatoes
¼	cup white wine (optional)

Preheat the oven to 350°F. In a bowl mix the flour with the salt and pepper. Dredge the chicken in the flour. Melt the 2 tablespoons butter in a heavy skillet and sauté the chicken on medium-high heat until golden brown. Remove and place in an ovenproof baking dish. Melt the remaining 4 tablespoons butter in a skillet and sauté the pepper, onion, celery, and garlic for several minutes. Add the mushrooms and sauté until the vegetables are tender but not brown. Remove the pan from the heat. Stir in the tomatoes and ¼ cup white wine. Pour the mixture over the chicken and bake for 20 to 25 minutes or until the chicken is done.

MAKES 4 SERVINGS

CRANBERRY GLAZED CHICKEN BREASTS

Jellied cranberry sauce is a secret passion of many aficionados of Thanksgiving dinner; the freshest, sweet-tartest cranberries from Cape Cod cannot substitute for the sugary red stuff that comes in a can. In this recipe, the otherwise cloying sauce is nicely tempered by salty soy and spices, giving the chicken breasts a shimmering flavor that goes bone-deep.

6	*chicken breast quarters*
	Salt and pepper
1	*(8-ounce) can jellied cranberry sauce*
¼	*cup soy sauce*
½	*cup packed brown sugar*
1	*teaspoon salt*
1	*teaspoon dry mustard*
1	*teaspoon ground ginger*
1	*clove garlic, crushed*
2	*tablespoons lemon juice*

Preheat the oven to 325°F. Place the chicken breasts in a broiling pan and slightly season with the salt and pepper. Cook for 1½ hours on the top rack of the oven.

For the glaze, in a saucepan combine the cranberry sauce, soy sauce, brown sugar, salt, dry mustard, ginger, garlic, and lemon juice. Heat to dissolve the sugar and liquefy the cranberry sauce. Baste the chicken with the glaze and cook another 30 minutes.

MAKES 6 SERVINGS

FRIED CHICKEN WITH CHICKEN-FRIED BISCUITS

Fried dough is a favorite Yankee treat that takes many forms: fritters to accompany chowder in Rhode Island, malasadas as part of a Portuguese seafood supper in New Bedford, and—quite simply—fried dough (topped with cinnamon sugar) to eat on the stroll at summer fairs. In that same spirit, the notion of frying biscuits to accompany chicken makes wonderful sense. While utterly iconoclastic by southern fried-chicken standards, Durgin-Park's way provides small spherical breadstuffs with a luscious crunch that sings harmony with well-fried chicken.

Chicken:		Biscuits:	
6	*chicken breast halves*	2	*cups all-purpose flour*
6	*chicken thighs*	1	*tablespoon baking powder*
2	*cups buttermilk*	1	*tablespoon sugar*
	Vegetable oil	½	*teaspoon salt*
1	*cup all-purpose flour*	1¼	*cups milk*
2	*teaspoons paprika*		
1	*teaspoon pepper*		
2	*teaspoons salt*		

Wash and dry the chicken pieces. In a shallow pan marinate the chicken pieces in the buttermilk for 4 hours, turning two or three times. Drain, discarding the buttermilk. In an electric skillet or fry pan, heat ½ inch of vegetable oil to 375°F. Place the flour, paprika, pepper, and salt in a plastic bag; add the chicken two or three pieces at a time and shake until well coated. Place the chicken pieces in the heated oil and fry. (Leave the skillet uncovered for crispy chicken.) Fry on each side for approximately 20 minutes, or until browned and crispy. Remove the chicken to an ovenproof platter and keep warm in the oven while you prepare the biscuits.

In a medium bowl whisk together the flour, baking powder, sugar, and salt. Stir in the milk with a fork and mix well—the mixture will be gooey. Heat the remaining oil in the skillet to 375°F. Drop the mixture by teaspoonfuls into the oil. Cook for about 4 minutes on each side until golden brown. Drain on paper towels. Serve with the chicken.

MAKES 6 SERVINGS

SAUTÉED CHICKEN LIVERS WITH MUSHROOMS

The combination of earthy mushrooms with luscious chicken livers, flavored with a dash of sherry, makes this dish sheer joy to eat. It's quick to cook, too . . . and easy on the wallet.

2	plus 2 tablespoons butter or vegetable oil
1	large onion, coarsely chopped
1	pound fresh mushrooms, coarsely sliced
1	pound chicken livers, trimmed, rinsed, and drained
⅓	cup dry sherry
¼	rounded teaspoon dried thyme or 2 teaspoons minced fresh thyme
	Dash of hot red pepper sauce
	Salt and pepper
¼	cup minced fresh parsley or chervil

In a large skillet heat 2 tablespoons butter or oil over medium heat; add the onions and mushrooms and sauté until the mushrooms begin to brown and all of their liquid has evaporated, about 10 to 15 minutes. Remove the mushroom mixture from the skillet with a slotted spoon to a medium bowl; set aside. In the same skillet heat the remaining 2 tablespoons butter or oil, add the chicken livers and brown over medium heat, turning once, cooking about 5 minutes on each side. Return the mushroom-onion mixture to the skillet; add the sherry, thyme, pepper sauce, and salt and pepper to taste. Simmer over medium-low heat for about 5 minutes to blend the flavors and cook off the alcohol. Remove from the heat and stir in the parsley or chervil. Serve immediately, or transfer the mixture to a serving dish and keep hot in a warm oven.

MAKES 4 SERVINGS

VERMONT ROAST TURKEY

You can have Thanksgiving dinner every day at Durgin-Park, where three fresh turkeys are cooked each weekday, and five or six each Saturday and Sunday. A complete meal includes not only turkey and dressing, but also mashed potatoes and gravy and a serving of butternut squash. And needless to say: corn bread to begin and Indian pudding to finish.

---

1   *turkey*
     Olive oil, butter, or cooking oil

Singe, clean, and rub the inside of the turkey with salt; stuff and truss. Rub the entire turkey well with olive oil, butter, or cooking oil. Place the breast side up in an ordinary dripping pan with a rack in the bottom. Do not cover. In such a roaster any steam that forms will go off into the air and not stay inside to draw juices from the turkey and make it dry.

    Roast the turkey at a moderately slow temperature (325°F). Do not sear. Keeping the temperature constant throughout the cooking gives a finished bird that is cooked evenly. There will be little or no sputtering, and the drippings will be just right for making a good brown gravy. Allow 25 to 30 minutes per pound. A young turkey weighing between 10 and 14 pounds, market weight, requires 3 to 3½ hours roasting. (Market weight means picked, but not drawn, and including the head and feet.) Turn a turkey cooked in an open roaster breast side down the last 30 minutes of roasting. To turn without breaking the skin, pick the turkey up by the neck and legs, using several folds of soft clean cloth to hold it. To determine if the turkey is done, run a steel skewer or cooking fork into the thickest part of the breast and also into the thigh next to the breast. If the meat is tender and the juice does not look red, the turkey is roasted enough. Basting is not necessary if the bird is fat; otherwise baste every 30 minutes with pan drippings or water and butter.

A 15-POUND TURKEY MAKES 20 GENEROUS SERVINGS

NEW ENGLAND PORK CHOPS

Nowadays, when traveling eaters think of a region in which to eat good pork, the South is what comes to mind. But there was a time when the New England landscape had plenty of farms, and every one had a few hogs on the property. Inland cookery was once replete with hams, pork roasts, and chops.

---

4   *pork chops, well trimmed*
    Flour
4   *medium-sized onions, sliced*
2   *tablespoons butter or vegetable shortening*
    Salt and pepper

Cover both sides of the pork chops with flour. Fry the onions in the butter until light brown. Place the chops in a skillet with the onions. Brown quickly on both sides; season with the salt and pepper to taste. Add water enough to cover and cook, tightly covered, over low flame for 45 minutes. Chops will be tender with a slightly thick brown gravy.

MAKES 2 TO 4 SERVINGS

BIG SERVINGS

Sᴍᴀʟʟ ᴘᴏʀᴛɪᴏɴs ᴀʀᴇ antithetical to the spirit of Durgin-Park. Even the modestly priced lunch specials, such as "Poor Man's Roast Beef," are sized for prosperous appetites, and the most basic sandwiches come overstuffed. Suppers of corned beef and cabbage, roast stuffed turkey with all the trimmings, and loin of pork (with homemade applesauce, of course) are immense, and the New England clambake dinner of chowder, steamers, lobster, potato, and corn-on-the-cob is a one-person picnic. The Durgin Cut prime rib is famously vast; its bone extending far off the plate. But the relatively smaller Yankee cut of prime rib will surely satisfy a Yankee-and-a-half. (Order-splitting is forbidden by the management, but carryout containers are gladly given for the inevitable leftovers.)

Desserts are particularly outsized, a tradition that goes back at least as far as pastry chef Martha Bence, who worked in the Durgin-Park kitchen for most of the first half of the twentieth century. It was Ms. Bence who made and personally sliced each serving of the kitchen's renowned apple pie. The legend says that Ms. Bence decided to retire in 1942 at the age of seventy, but

her retirement was plagued by horrible dreams—nightmares in which she saw her replacements in the Durgin-Park kitchen cutting apple pie into bite-sized portions and serving it to hungry customers in sewing thimbles. After three weeks away she returned to Durgin-Park to ensure that the pie was cut the way it was supposed to be cut, in wedges that are nearly one-quarter pie apiece.

The legendary generosity of Durgin-Park is especially conspicuous because in so many ways it is a no-nonsense restaurant that reflects a spirit of Downeast frugality. No money is squandered on décor, entertainment, or frivolous amenities. China and silver are functional. Lighting is harsh. The staff's uniforms are institutional. You won't find a lot of sprigs or sprinkles of anything on your plate just for pretty effect. But when the meal is set before you, such trivia is immaterial. What matters is that your plate is covered with Thanksgiving-sized portions of expertly made Yankee food.

PAPRIKA PORK ROAST

This slow-cooked roast yields a hunk of pork that wants to fall apart as soon as you touch it with your carving knife. It's great with simple mashed potatoes, but when we want a meal that has a broader range of flavors, we like to serve it with Durgin-Park's Parmesan Potato Rounds (p. 85).

2	teaspoons garlic salt
1	teaspoon ground ginger
1	teaspoon pepper
1	teaspoon paprika
1	boneless, rolled, pork loin roast (4 to 4½ pounds)
1	or 2 medium onions, sliced
1	cup water

Preheat the oven to 325°F. Combine the garlic salt, ginger, pepper, and paprika; rub over the entire roast. Place the roast with fat side up on a greased rack in a roasting pan. Top with the onion slices. Pour the water into the pan. Roast uncovered for 2 to 2½ hours or until a meat thermometer reads 160°F.

MAKES 10 SERVINGS

ROASTED PORK LOIN

The flavors that are infused into the meat in this recipe are bold and seductive but not so much that they overwhelm the succulence of slow-cooked pork. That is because pork loin, while it is an impressionable food that loves to assume the flavors of what surrounds it, tends to keep its fundamental porcine character.

½	cup finely chopped onion
½	cup finely chopped celery
½	cup finely chopped green pepper
3	tablespoons butter or margarine
6	garlic cloves, minced
1	teaspoon salt
1	teaspoon pepper
1	teaspoon onion powder
1	teaspoon dried thyme
1	teaspoon paprika
1	teaspoon ground mustard
½	teaspoon garlic powder
1	boneless pork loin roast (4 to 5 pounds)

In a skillet combine the onion, celery, green pepper, butter, garlic, salt, pepper, onion powder, thyme, paprika, mustard, and garlic powder. Sauté the mixture until the vegetables are tender. Preheat the oven to 325°F. Randomly cut 20 deep slits, 1-inch wide, on the inside surface of the roast. Fill the slits with some of the vegetable mixture and tie the roast together with some twine. Place on a rack in a shallow baking pan. Spread the remaining vegetable mixture over the roast. Bake uncovered for 2 to 3 hours or until a meat thermometer reads 160°F to 170°F.

MAKES 10 TO 12 SERVINGS

STUFFED PORK CHOPS

Stuffing is big in the New England kitchen, and not only in the holiday turkey. Lobsters, shrimp, and flatfish are embellished with it at every deluxe seafood restaurant, and the old favorite, pork chops, is often served double-thick and filled with moist stuffing that is flavored by the juices of the pork as it cooks. Long ago, when Durgin-Park served breakfast, pork chops with applesauce was on the breakfast menu—a hearty repast for men who had been up working in the market since the early morning hours.

Pork Chops:		Stuffing:	
6	double-thick loin pork chops	1½	cups bread crumbs
¾	cup all-purpose flour	½	cup finely chopped celery
1½	teaspoons salt	¼	cup finely chopped onion
	Pepper	3	tablespoons melted butter
4	to 6 tablespoons vegetable oil	1	tablespoon minced parsley
		1	teaspoon rosemary, crushed
		1	to 1½ cups chicken broth
			Salt and pepper

Make a pocket in each pork chop by slicing into the side ¾ way in toward the bone. Mix the flour with the salt and pepper to taste and dredge the pork chops in the flour. In a large skillet heat the oil over medium heat and brown the chops on both sides until golden brown, about 20 minutes. Set aside.

To prepare the stuffing, brown the bread crumbs in the same skillet and transfer them to a medium bowl. Add the celery, onion, butter, parsley, and rosemary. Moisten with the chicken broth just enough to hold the mixture together. Salt and pepper to taste. Preheat the oven to 300°F. Fill the pockets of the pork chops with the stuffing and close each one with a toothpick. They may close only partially, and some stuffing will fall out, but that's okay. Place in a 9 x 13-inch baking dish and add 1 cup chicken broth. Cover tightly with a lid or foil and bake in the oven for 3 hours, basting every 45 minutes. Add more broth if the pan starts to dry up.

MAKES 6 SERVINGS

BAKED HAM

Early in the twentieth century, ham roast with spinach was an everyday dinner at Durgin-Park, where it sold for fifty cents, including mashed potatoes and bread and butter (a nickel extra for sweet potatoes). Today, most people think of a whole ham as a party food. It requires some time and effort to cook, but the results are a delicious meal with leftovers for days, plus a bone for making Ham and Pea Soup (p. 44) or Purée of Split Pea Soup (p. 45).

1	*(5- to 6-pound) ham, fully cooked*
¾	*cup fresh orange juice*
½	*cup dry sherry*
1	*cup honey*
	Whole cloves
1	*cup packed, dark brown sugar*
2	*tablespoons ground mustard*

Trim the skin from the ham, leaving a thin, even layer of fat. With a skewer, poke the ham all over at 2-inch intervals. Place the ham in a large, resealable plastic bag, and place in a large shallow pan. In a small bowl combine the orange juice, sherry, and honey; pour over the ham and seal the bag securely. Marinate in the refrigerator for three days, turning the ham every 12 hours.

Preheat the oven to 325°F. Remove the ham from the bag, reserving the marinade. In a shallow roasting pan, with the ham fat side up, score the fat in a diamond design and stud with cloves. Insert a meat thermometer, making sure it does not touch the bone. Pour all but one tablespoon of the marinade over the ham. Bake for 1½ hours or until the meat thermometer registers 130°F. In a small bowl combine the brown sugar, mustard, and the tablespoon of reserved marinade and brush the exposed portion of the ham. Cover with a tent of aluminum foil and bake for an additional 15 minutes or until the meat thermometer registers 140°F. Remove from the oven and allow the meat to stand for 10 minutes; then slice thinly and serve.

MAKES 10 TO 12 SERVINGS

HAM BAKED IN CIDER

The combination of maple syrup and apple cider is 100 percent Yankee . . . and an unbeatable way to glaze a thick slice of ham.

1½   *pound center slice of smoked ham, cut 2 inches thick*
15   *whole cloves*
2   *tablespoons dry mustard*
½   *cup maple syrup*
½   *cup cider (or apple juice)*

Preheat the oven to 350°F. Stick the whole cloves into the fat and rub the mustard over the ham. Lay in a casserole and pour the maple syrup and cider over the ham. Bake until tender, about 1½ hours.

MAKES 3 SERVINGS

HAM AND NOODLE CASSEROLE

What cooks of the Great Plains would call a "hot dish," this hearty casserole reminds us of church suppers and block parties. In fact, it's a handy recipe to have in the days after Easter or Christmas, when leftover ham weighs heavy in the kitchen inventory.

8	*ounces wide noodles*
¼	*cup margarine*
1	*medium onion, chopped*
2	*eggs, beaten*
½	*cup sour cream*
2	*cups diced ham*
¼	*teaspoon salt*
¼	*teaspoon pepper*
¼	*cup bread crumbs*
	Paprika

Cook the noodles for only 3 minutes; let them stand for 10 minutes before draining. Preheat the oven to 350°F. Stir the margarine and the onion into the noodles. In a separate bowl stir the eggs into the sour cream. Then combine the egg mixture, ham, salt, and pepper with the noodles. Sprinkle the bread crumbs into a 2-quart casserole. Top with the noodle mixture. Sprinkle with the paprika and bake uncovered until set, 40 to 50 minutes.

MAKES 4 TO 6 SERVINGS

MAINE CORNED BEEF HASH

When making corned beef hash, most cooks advise putting it in the skillet (preferably a heavy cast-iron one), patting it down, then not disturbing it at all until the bottom is good and crusty.

3   cups boiled potatoes
4   cups corned beef
¼   cup butter
¾   cup boiling water
     Pepper

Place the cold potatoes and cold corned beef (free from gristle and fat) in a chopping bowl. Chop until both meat and potatoes are in very small pieces. Melt the butter in a heavy skillet. Add the boiling water. Add the chopped meat and potatoes seasoned with the pepper. Fry over very low heat for about 15 minutes, or until a brown crust has formed on lower side of hash; then fold over as an omelet is folded.

MAKES 4 TO 6 SERVINGS

RED FLANNEL HASH

Hash used to be a dirty word, and to call a restaurant a "hash house" still has an unsavory connotation. That's because diners of yore used to make hash out of any old scraps that appeared in the kitchen, including mystery meat of unknown provenance. But the fact is that well-made hash, created out of leftovers, is one of the great blue-plate meals of the American kitchen. It is especially typical of New England kitchens because it is a waste-not dish, made from yesterday's corned beef.

Durgin-Park's version is the kind generally known as red flannel hash, taking advantage of leftovers from a traditional boiled dinner, including not only corned beef and potatoes, but also enough beets to dye the dish a deep pink color reminiscent of comfortable old flannel pj's.

1	tablespoon butter
1	cup chopped, cooked corned beef
3	cups chopped boiled potatoes
1	cup chopped cooked beets
½	onion, chopped

Heat the butter in a frying pan. Mix together the corned beef, potatoes, beets, and onion. Spread the mixture smoothly over the bottom of the pan. Brown slowly. When a crust forms, turn as an omelet.

MAKES 4 SERVINGS

VERMONT CORNED BEEF

To "corn" something means to pickle or preserve it using salt that is finely ground (once known as "corn ground"). In the days before refrigeration, beef was preserved by keeping it in a crock full of brine. This recipe doesn't require you to do that. Simply buy an already-corned beef at the supermarket. As is true for nearly every other recipe that calls for maple syrup as a cooking ingredient, don't use the fancy grade A stuff; it doesn't have the flavor oomph you want.

4	or 5 pounds corned beef
	Whole cloves
½	cup maple syrup

Cover the corned beef with water and bring to a boil. Drain and cover with hot water; let simmer until done, allowing about 40 minutes per pound. When done, place the meat on a rack in an open roasting pan. Preheat the oven to 350°F. Stick with the whole cloves in a diagonal design. Pour the maple syrup over the meat and put it in the oven to brown and glaze. Baste occasionally with the maple syrup.

MAKES 4 TO 6 SERVINGS

MEAT LOAF

Durgin-Park's recipe for meat loaf should be made with hamburger meat (ground chuck or sirloin) that is no more than 20 percent fat, no less than 10 percent. Although the time-honored formula likely originated as a way to stretch the meat supply, most meat-loaf lovers—even those who have no need or desire to pinch pennies—would have it no other way. The cup of breadcrumbs gives this loaf of meat a well-built character that connoisseurs of institutional cooking find irresistible. One good reason for making it is that meat loaf also demands making plenty of mashed potatoes.

2	pounds hamburger
1	cup bread crumbs
1	onion, chopped
2	eggs
½	cup plus 2 tablespoons ketchup
¼	cup milk
2	teaspoons salt
¼	teaspoon pepper

Preheat the oven to 375°F. Combine the hamburger, bread crumbs, onion, eggs, ½ cup ketchup, milk, salt, and pepper. Put into a greased loaf pan and spread the remaining 2 tablspoons ketchup on top. Bake for 1 to 1½ hours.

MAKES 8 TO 10 SERVINGS

SPAGHETTI AND MEATBALL DINNER

Boston's North End is probably the most spaghetti-conscious neighborhood in America. The Prince's Spaghetti Company used to run advertisements that proclaimed, "Wednesday Is Prince Spaghetti Day," and showed young Bostonians running home for a big, traditional spaghetti and meatball dinner.

Meatballs:		Spaghetti Sauce:	
1	pound lean ground beef	1	to 2 teaspoons olive oil
¼	teaspoon coarsely ground pepper	2	(1-inch-thick) rib-end pork chops
1	teaspoon salt	4	(6-ounce) cans tomato paste
1	garlic clove, finely minced	8	cups defatted chicken broth
2	tablespoons finely minced parsley	1	teaspoon salt
¾	cup packed, freshly grated Parmesan cheese	½	teaspoon freshly ground pepper
1½	cups dry bread crumbs	1	tablespoon dried basil, or ½ cup chopped fresh
4	large eggs		Bit of sugar
2	tablespoons olive oil	2	pounds thin spaghetti (spaghettini)

To make the meatballs, combine the beef, pepper, salt, garlic, and parsley in a large bowl. Add the cheese, bread crumbs, and eggs and blend. Mix well and form into large marble-sized balls. In a large skillet heat the oil and brown the meatballs on all sides. Drain them on paper towels when done.

To make the sauce, heat the oil in a medium skillet and brown the pork chops on both sides; set aside. In a large, deep kettle combine the tomato paste, broth, salt, and pepper with a whisk. Add the pork chops and the pan drippings to the sauce. Bring the mixture to a boil, reduce the heat, and simmer, partially covered, for 1½ hours, stirring frequently. Add the meatballs and basil and continue cooking for 30 minutes or until the sauce reaches the desired consistency. Add more broth if necessary. If desired sprinkle in a bit of sugar to soften the sharp tomato flavor. Remove the pork chops and either discard them or mince the meat and return to the sauce.

Cook the spaghetti according to package directions, adding 2 tablespoons of oil to the cooking water to prevent the spaghetti from clumping together. Drain well and serve the hot sauce and meatballs over the hot spaghetti.

MAKES 12 TO 16 SERVINGS

POTTED BEEF SMOTHERED ONIONS

Similar in nature to a dish known down east as *stifled beef,* potted beef is a regular lunch item on the Durgin-Park menu. It's a hearty meal using inexpensive cuts of beef . . . or left-over roast beef.

4	to 5 pounds braising beef, either flap meat or flank steak
6	to 8 carrots, chopped
6	onions, chopped
1	(3-pound) can stewed tomatoes
1	bunch celery, chopped
6	teaspoons celery salt
6	teaspoons black pepper
6	bay leaves
8	ounces beef stock
1	(12-ounce) bottle steak sauce

Preheat the oven to 400°F. Flour the meat, and place in a roasting pan; braise for 30 minutes, or until the meat is browned. Remove from the oven and place in a stockpot. Cover with water and add the carrots, onions, tomatoes, celery, celery salt, black pepper, bay leaves, beef base, and steak sauce. Bring to a boil and then simmer for 1½ hours or until the meat is fork tender.

MAKES 8 TO 10 SERVINGS

SHORT RIBS OF BEEF

Short ribs deliver maximum flavor for minimum cost, but you really need to love beef to enjoy them. And when we say *love beef,* we are referring to the part of the beef that makes it taste good, which is the fat. There is no way around the fact that short ribs are a fatty food. But those who love them prefer to think of that quality as succulence—a combination of flavor and tenderness that a blue-ribbon filet mignon cannot deliver.

6	to 8 pounds beef short ribs
	Flour
	Salt and pepper
6	celery ribs, chopped
3	medium onions, chopped
4	carrots, chopped
6	garlic cloves, chopped
1	(3-pound) can stewed tomatoes
8	teaspoons celery salt
8	teaspoons black pepper
6	to 8 bay leaves
5	ounces A-1 sauce
12	ounces beef stock

Preheat the oven to 375°F. Flour the ribs and place it in a large roasting pan; sprinkle with the salt and pepper to taste. Place the seasoned ribs in a casserole and bake for 1 to 1½ hours, or until the ribs are browned. When done remove the ribs from the oven and place them in a large stockpot. Add the celery, onions, carrots, garlic, stewed tomatoes, celery salt, black pepper, bay leaves, A-1 sauce, and beef base. Cover the ingredients with water. Bring to a boil; then reduce the heat and simmer for approximately 1 to 1½ hours or until the meat is fork tender. When done remove the pot from the stove and let it sit for 5 to 10 minutes before serving.

MAKES 6 TO 8 SERVINGS

YANKEE POT ROAST

There was a time, not so long ago, when only grandmothers prepared pot roast. In recent years, as American cooks and eaters have come to appreciate the joys of comfort food, the dowdy old dish has earned a new lease on life. Of course, the kitchens of Durgin-Park never stopped making it.

4	to 5 pounds pot roast (brisket or cap meat)
	Flour for dredging
6	carrots, chopped
2	small onions
6	celery ribs
1	(3-pound) can stewed tomatoes
2	tablespoons celery salt
2	tablespoons white pepper
6	bay leaves
1	teaspoon poultry seasoning
5	ounces A-1 sauce
6	ounces beef stock
	Flour
	Water

Preheat the oven to 400°F. Dredge the pot roast in the flour, place the meat in a roasting pan, and cook in the oven for 1 hour, browning all sides. Once browned, place the meat in a large stock pot or a Dutch oven. Cover with water. Add the carrots, onions, celery, tomatoes, celery salt, white pepper, poultry seasoning, A-1 sauce, and beef base. Simmer on top of the stove or in the oven at 325°F. Cook for approximately 2 hours or until the meat is tender. Strain the liquid. Make a paste out of equal amounts of flour and water and add to the liquid to make the gravy. Serve with boiled or mashed potatoes.

MAKES 10 TO 12 SERVINGS

OVEN SWISS STEAK

Few recipes are less glamorous than Swiss steak. But for those who appreciate a characterful cut of beef deeply flavored by the natural sweetness of vegetables, the primest of prime beef could never substitute for this satisfying dish.

1½	*pounds top round steak, cut ¾-inch thick*
¼	*cup flour*
1	*teaspoon salt*
2	*tablespoons shortening*
1	*(16-ounce) can stewed tomatoes*
½	*cup chopped celery*
½	*cup chopped carrots*
2	*tablespoons chopped onion*
½	*teaspoon Worcestershire sauce*
¼	*cup shredded American cheese*

Preheat the oven to 350°F. Cut the meat into four portions. Mix together the flour and salt and pound into the meat. Set aside any remaining flour. In a skillet heat the shortening and brown the meat before placing in a shallow casserole. Blend the remaining flour with the meat drippings. Add the tomatoes, celery, carrots, onion, and Worcestershire sauce. Cook on medium-high, stirring constantly, until the mixture boils. Pour the sauce over the meat. Cover and bake for 2 hours or until tender. Top with the cheese, and return to the oven for a few minutes.

MAKES 6 TO 8 SERVINGS

PERFECT ROAST BEEF

Durgin-Park is known for beef. Chef Tommy Ryan, who began his career as a butcher, is proud of the fact that he doesn't buy portion-controlled steaks and roasts ready to cook. He breaks down prime cuts into everything from sirloin steak to hamburger. Recently, when sandwiches were added to the lunch menu, roast beef was a featured attraction.

1	*(6-pound) boneless beef rib roast, tied*
1	*cup flour*
4	*teaspoons finely minced onion*
4	*teaspoons finely minced garlic*
4	*teaspoons minced parsley*
½	*teaspoon dried thyme or 1½ teaspoons fresh minced thyme*
	Salt and coarsely ground pepper

Let the roast sit for approximately 1 hour to allow it to come to room temperature. Preheat the oven to 350°F. In a bowl combine the flour, onion, garlic, parsley, thyme, and pepper. Mix thoroughly and rub over the rib roast. Place the roast in a roasting pan and bake for 1½ hours. Let the roast sit for about 30 minutes before serving.

MAKES 12 SERVINGS

LAMB STEAKS

While lamb is not nearly as popular as it once was on restaurant menus, Durgin-Park currently offers it three ways: roast leg of lamb, broiled lamb chops, and broiled lamb steak. You can also get a mixed grill that includes lamb kidney.

1	*bay leaf*
1	*teaspoon finely chopped thyme*
1	*teaspoon finely chopped parsley*
1	*teaspoon finely chopped sweet marjoram*
1	*teaspoon finely chopped mint*
1	*teaspoon salt*
1	*teaspoon pepper*
4	*lamb chops (loin, center cut, or shoulder), cut thick*
	Olive oil
1	*teaspoon dry mustard*

Pulverize the bay leaf. Mix with the thyme, parsley, marjoram, and mint about an hour before cooking the meat. Salt and pepper the chops and broil on both sides. Mix the olive oil with the herbs and dry mustard to make a paste. When the chops are very hot, spread each one with a mixture of the olive oil and herbs. Serve at once.

MAKES 4 SERVINGS

NEW ENGLAND BOILED DINNER

When it comes to eating plain and square, New England can't be beat; a New England boiled dinner is the plainest, squarest, clunkiest meal of them all. Picture it: a hunk of corned beef brisket striated with juicy veins of fat, falling-into-shreds tender, sliced thick, in the center of a big oval platter. Around this great meat hub glistens a faded rainbow of vegetables: limp cabbage wedges, steamy and pale; white boiled potatoes; and heavy hunks of turnip. Above this hot rugged landscape hovers a cloud of briny perfume. With a glass of cider, hard or sweet, this is the primary Yankee meal, and perhaps the most basic plate of food in America. If you doubt this fact, consider its name: *Boiled Dinner*. It could not sound more fundamental unless you called it *Dinner, Boiled*.

5	to 6 pound gray corned beef brisket
4	to 6 bay leaves
6	to 8 potatoes, quartered
1	turnip, coarsely cut
6	to 8 carrots, chopped
1	head cabbage, quartered

Place the brisket in a large pot and cover it with water; add the bay leaves. Bring to a boil; then reduce the heat and simmer for approximately 3 hours. Add the potatoes, turnips, and carrots during the last hour. Add the cabbage during the last 15 to 20 minutes. Remember to slice the corned beef across the grain of the meat when serving.

[Note: To cure your own corned beef, buy a fresh piece of brisket. Make a brine by mixing 1 pound kosher salt and 1 gallon water. Cover the meat with the brine and refrigerate for 48 to 72 hours.]

MAKES 10 TO 12 SERVINGS

DEEP FRIED FOODS

No state in the union is prouder of its fried seafood than Massachusetts. On the North Shore, less than an hour from Boston, several restaurants feature menus that serve virtually nothing other than fried seafood accompanied by fried potatoes, fried onions, and fried fritters, too!

6	*eggs*
3	*cups whole milk*
3	*cups all-purpose flour*
1½	*cups yellow corn flour*
1½	*pounds haddock*
	Vegetable oil

Make an egg wash by beating in a bowl the eggs and milk. In a separate bowl combine the all-purpose flour and the corn flour. Cut the haddock into four equal filets. Soak the haddock filets in the egg wash. Then dredge them in the flour and deep fry them in a hot pan with enough vegetable oil to cover the fish. Fry until the breading is brown and crispy, about 8 to 10 minutes.

[Note: You may substitute just about any other type of fish (clams, scallops, shrimp, or sole) or onions.]

MAKES 4 SERVINGS

• DESSERTS •

APPLE OR BLUEBERRY CRISP

The goodness of a crisp depends on the taste of its fruit. In the summer, when tart, full-flavored blueberries become available, that's the way to go. In autumn, use apples at their peak. Either way, serve your crisp warm . . . and preferably with a scoop of vanilla, pumpkin, ginger, or Grape-Nuts ice cream (vanilla ice cream streaked with softened Grape-Nuts cereal).

¼	plus ⅓ cup butter, softened
4	cups cored and sliced apples or fresh blueberries
¼	cup water
1	teaspoon cinnamon
½	teaspoon salt
1	cup sugar
¾	cup flour

Preheat the oven to 350°F. Lightly grease a 10 x 10-inch pan with ¼ cup of butter. Place the apples (or berries) in the greased pan. Sprinkle the water, cinnamon, and salt over the top. Cut the remaining ⅓ cup butter into the sugar and flour and spread over the fruit. Bake for 40 minutes.

MAKES 4 TO 6 SERVINGS

APPLE BROWN BETTY

Yankee desserts have arcane names. This is a land of pandowdies, grunts, duffs, slumps, buckles, and brown Betties. A brown Betty should be nicely browned in the oven, which explains the first part of its name, but no one seems to know why it is called Betty.

¼	cup butter
2	cups fresh bread crumbs
6	cups cored, peeled, thinly sliced apples
½	cup light brown sugar
1	tablespoon lemon juice
1	teaspoon ground cinnamon
½	teaspoon ground allspice
½	teaspoon ground nutmeg
⅓	cup apple cider

Preheat the oven to 375°F. Melt the butter in a saucepan, add the crumbs and mix thoroughly. Grease a deep, 2-quart baking dish. Sprinkle a few bread crumbs on the bottom of the dish. Arrange half of the apples on top of the crumbs. Sprinkle with half of the sugar, half of the lemon juice, half of the spices. Then add half of the remaining bread crumbs. Repeat the layers and pour the cider over the finished arrangement. Top with the remaining bread crumbs. Cover and bake for 45 minutes. Remove the cover and test with a knife to see if the apples are cooked. If need be, cook a little longer uncovered. Do not overcook or the Betty will collapse.

MAKES 6 TO 8 SERVINGS

APPLE CAKE

Among the provisions carried by the Pilgrims who arrived at Plymouth Rock were apple seeds, and New England food authority Brooke Dojny wrote that "some of America's first apple orchards [were] planted on the slope of what would become Boston's Beacon Hill."

1½	cups oil
2	cups sugar
3	eggs
3	cups flour
1	teaspoon salt
1	teaspoon cinnamon
1	teaspoon baking soda
1	teaspoon vanilla
3	cups peeled, cored, thickly sliced, Red Delicious apples
1	cup chopped walnuts

Preheat the oven to 350°F. Grease and flour a tube pan. Beat the oil and sugar together in an electric mixer while assembling the remaining ingredients. Add the eggs and beat until creamy. Mix together the flour, salt, cinnamon, and baking soda. Stir the mixture by hand into the batter. Add the vanilla, apples, and nuts. Stir to blend. Turn into the pan. Bake for 1 hour 15 minutes or until done. Cool in the pan.

MAKES 1 TUBE CAKE

APPLE-CRANBERRY PIE

An autumn classic well-suited to the holiday table, but welcome any day. The sweet-tart combination of apples and cranberries is especially well-gilded by a scoop of vanilla or coffee ice cream.

Crust:

2	*cups all-purpose flour*
¼	*teaspoon salt*
½	*cup plus 1 tablespoon cold vegetable shortening*
4	*tablespoons cold butter, cut into ½ inch pieces*
¼	*cup ice water*

Filling:

6	*large Golden Delicious apples, peeled, halved, cored and each cut into 8 wedges*
1	*cup fresh or frozen cranberries*
2	*teaspoons finely grated orange zest*
1	*cup sugar*
3	*tablespoons all-purpose flour*
⅛	*teaspoon salt*
1	*large egg, beaten*
1	*tablespoon milk*

To make the pie crust, in a large bowl combine the flour and salt. Using a pastry cutter or two knives, cut the shortening and butter into the flour until it resembles coarse meal. Refrigerate the mixture for a few minutes if the butter becomes too soft. Drizzle the ice water over the flour mixture and, using a wooden spoon, stir just until the dough can be gathered into a ball. Divide the dough in half and pat each piece into a 6-inch disk. Wrap each disk in plastic wrap and refrigerate until firm, at least 2 hours or overnight, before using.

Preheat the oven to 400°F. Roll each disk of dough into a 12-inch round. Line a Pot Shop Earthenware Deep Dish Pie Plate with 1 round of dough and refrigerate both it and the second round until ready to fill.

To make the filling, in a large bowl toss together the apples, cranberries, orange zest, sugar, flour, and salt; transfer the mixture to the pie shell. In a separate bowl beat together the egg and milk to make an egg wash. Brush the edges of the pie shell with the egg wash and cover with the second dough round, lightly pressing the edges together. Leave enough overhanging dough, about 1 inch, to fold under. Crimp to seal. Brush the top crust with egg wash, avoiding the decorative rim as it tends to brown more quickly. Make four small slits in the top crust for venting. Set the pie on the middle shelf of the oven and place a baking sheet on the lower shelf to catch any drips. Bake the pie for about 1 hour or until the crust is light golden and the juices bubble. Cover the pie loosely with foil during the last 15 minutes to prevent excessive browning. Allow the pie to cool for 20 minutes; serve while warm.

MAKES 1 PIE

APPLE PANDOWDY

Variations of apple pie abound in Yankee cookery. Pandowdy—which has all the ingredients of apple pie, plus molasses, is traditionally made in a square pan with crust at the top and bottom. Speculation about the origin of its name runs in two directions: it's *dowdy,* meaning "homely," or its crust is *dowdied* (broken into pieces) before it is served.

10	Courtland apples, sliced
1	cup molasses
1	cup sugar
1	cup water
1	teaspoon cloves
1	teaspoon cinnamon
	Biscuit crust

Fill a heavy pot heaping full of the apples. Add the molasses, sugar, water, cloves, and cinnamon. Cover with a baking powder biscuit crust, sloping it over the sides. Bake overnight (10 to 12 hours). In the morning, cut the hard crust into the apples.

MAKES 4 TO 6 SERVINGS

APPLE PIE

Once you've eaten Durgin-Park apple pie, most others pale by comparison. Served in great big slices, it has no secret ingredients, for it is a classic. The one element that is crucial is the lard crust. Of course, you won't go to jail if you make your crust with vegetable shortening instead, but your pie will lack the dreamy combination of delicacy and intensely satisfying flavor that only lard can deliver.

⅔	*cup lard*
2	*cups flour*
1½	*teaspoons salt*
¼	*cup cold water*
6	*to 8 tart apples*
1	*cup sugar*
	Cinnamon
	Nutmeg
2	*tablespoons butter*
2	*tablespoons heavy cream*

Preheat the oven to 450°F. In a medium bowl mix the lard, flour, and salt. Pour the water over the mixture, gradually working it in with a fork. Divide it into two parts for the upper and lower crust. Peel, core, and slice the apples. Fill a 9-inch deep pan to slightly rounding. Pour the sugar on top of the apples. Add a shake of the cinnamon and nutmeg. Dot the apples with small pieces of the butter. Shake a speck of salt over the top. Moisten the edges of the bottom crust and add the top layer. Crimp the edges. Gloss the crust with the heavy cream. Bake the apples for 15 to 20 minutes. Reduce the heat to 350°F and bake for 35 to 40 minutes longer.

MAKES 6 TO 8 SERVINGS

APPLESAUCE CAKE

This spicy-sweet cake makes a wonderful snack or breakfast pastry. While Durgin-Park uses its own applesauce, which is begun by peeling and coring apples one by one on a vintage hand-crank peeler, it is perfectly okay to use store-bought in this recipe.

1	cup sugar
½	cup shortening
1	cup warm applesauce
1	teaspoon baking soda
1⅔	cups flour, sifted
1	teaspoon cinnamon
½	teaspoon ground cloves
¼	teaspoon nutmeg
¼	teaspoon salt
1	cup raisins, floured

Preheat the oven to 325°F. In a bowl cream the sugar and shortening. Add the applesauce to the sugar mixture. Dissolve the baking soda and add to the applesauce mixture. In another bowl mix together the flour, cinnamon, cloves, nutmeg, and salt and add to the applesauce mixture along with the raisins. Turn into a greased loaf pan and bake for about 45 minutes.

MAKES 1 CAKE

CAKE POEM

I**F YOU'VE EVER** hung around with an old Yankee cook, you might have heard this verse or a version of it. No one knows who wrote it or when, but it's heard often among the old-time bakers down east of Boston.

I baked a cake, and my, it was good!
It rose and it browned as all cakes should.
I made some tea, fragrant and strong.
But that day, no one came along.

I made a cake and it was punk:
It rose and then it went kerplunk.
I made some tea, both weak and thin.
And that day all our friends dropped in!

APPLE UPSIDE-DOWN CAKE

In her definitive book *Cooking Down East*, Marjorie Standish wrote, "We've a cake for every season in Maine. Maybe we don't make more kinds of cakes using fruits and berries than anywhere else, but it seems as if we do." Not only in Maine, but throughout New England, cakes have always been a fundamental part of the dessert repertoire. Even Beantown's best-known dessert, Boston cream pie, is, in fact, a cake! This upside-down cake calls for Golden Delicious apples, but feel free to experiment with other apples. Baking apples will give it a more tart, fruity character.

⅓	cup packed light brown sugar
2	plus 6 tablespoons margarine or butter, softened
3	medium Golden Delicious apples, peeled, cored, and cut into ¼-inch-thick wedges
1	cup all-purpose flour
1	teaspoon baking powder
¼	teaspoon salt
⅔	cup sugar
1	egg
1	teaspoon vanilla
⅓	cup milk

In a 12-inch skillet, heat the brown sugar with the 2 tablespoons butter over medium heat until melted, stirring occasionally. Add the apples and cook over high heat for 7 to 8 minutes or until the apples are fork-tender and beginning to brown. Transfer to a 9-inch, glass pie platter. Preheat the oven to 325°F. In a mixing bowl combine the flour, baking powder, and salt. In a separate large bowl, with the mixer at high speed, beat the remaining 6 tablespoons butter with the sugar until creamy, about 4 minutes, scraping the bowl often. Reduce the speed to low; add the egg and vanilla. With a rubber spatula, alternately fold in the flour mixture and milk, beginning and ending with the flour mixture. Spread the batter over the apples. Bake for 40 to 45 minutes or until a toothpick inserted in the center of the cake comes out clean. Immediately loosen the edge of the cake from the pie plate with the tip of a knife; invert the cake onto a serving plate. Serve warm.

MAKES 1 CAKE

BAKED INDIAN PUDDING

Durgin-Park's Indian pudding is the best there is. Dark brown with substantial gravity, it smells like roasted corn and tastes like the first Thanksgiving. The long cooking time is necessary to soften the corn and for the flavors to meld. Although some restaurants add raisins or other flavorings, the only traditional way to doll it up is with a scoop of vanilla ice cream melting fast atop each hot serving. Tommy Ryan loves telling the story about the time he was eating in a restaurant in New Hampshire—just a regular customer, unknown to the staff. He asked the waitress if they had Indian pudding for dessert. "Well, we do," she said reluctantly, but then she bent close and clued him in to a secret: "Sir, if you want really good Indian pudding, I suggest you go to Durgin-Park."

Just to keep the record straight: this is *not* a Native American dish adapted by colonist cooks. Its name comes from the fact that early settlers considered virtually anything made with corn to be Indian in nature.

1½	plus 1½ cups milk
¼	cup black molasses
2	tablespoons sugar
2	tablespoons butter
¼	teaspoon salt
⅛	teaspoon baking powder
1	egg
½	cup yellow cornmeal

Preheat the oven to 450°F. In a bowl mix 1½ cups of the milk with the molasses, sugar, butter, salt, baking powder, egg, and cornmeal. Pour the mixture into a stone crock that has been well greased and bake until it boils. Heat and stir in the remaining 1½ cups milk. Lower the oven temperature to 300°F and bake for 5 to 7 hours. Serve warm with whipped cream or vanilla ice cream.

MAKES 4 TO 6 SERVINGS

BANANA MUFFINS

What to do with those bananas that are getting a little too soft and speckled to eat? Mash them up and make them into muffins. Serve the muffins warm with plenty of softened butter to melt into them. If you make muffins one day and have some left over the next, carefully slice them in half and grill the halves until slightly crisp in a very well-buttered skillet.

⅓	cup shortening
⅔	cup sugar
2¾	teaspoons baking powder
½	teaspoon salt
2	eggs, beaten
1⅓	cups flour
1	cup mashed bananas
½	cup chopped nuts

Preheat the oven to 350°F. Beat the shortening and sugar until glossy, adding the sugar gradually. Add the baking powder, salt, and eggs and beat until thick. Alternately add the flour and bananas; add the nuts. Pour into greased muffin pans. Bake for 18 to 20 minutes.

MAKES 8 MUFFINS

BLUEBERRY CAKE

Not all blueberries are alike. Generally speaking, the smaller the blueberry, the more flavor it will have. The smallest and tastiest ones are the low-bush berries from Maine, which give this cake a surprising tang. While it can be served as dessert or an anytime snack, it is especially good served warm in the morning with hot coffee.

¾	cup sugar
2	eggs, beaten
3	cups flour
3	teaspoons baking powder
¾	teaspoon salt
1¼	cups blueberries, washed and drained
1	tablespoon melted butter
1½	cups milk

Preheat the oven to 400°F. In a bowl mix the sugar with the beaten eggs. Sift the flour, baking powder, and salt and add to the egg mixture. Stir in the blueberries, melted butter, and milk. Beat just enough to mix and pour into a 13 x 9 x 3-inch pan. Bake about 30 minutes.

MAKES 21 3-INCH X 2-INCH SQUARES

BLUEBERRY PIE

The voracity of New England's sweet tooth is second only to that of the South. Despite the stereotype of the dour Yankee character, this is a region that savors dessert in the form of puddings, crisps, Betties, grunts, and pies galore. In this recipe, wild blueberries from Maine are the best because they pack the most berry flavor.

1	cup sugar
¼	cup all-purpose flour
½	teaspoon finely shredded lemon peel
	Dash of salt
5	cups fresh blueberries or 1 (20-ounce) package frozen, unsweetened blueberries, thawed
	Pastry for double crust pie
2	teaspoons lemon juice
1	tablespoon butter or margarine

Preheat the oven to 375°F. In a mixing bowl combine the sugar, flour, lemon peel, and salt. Add the sugar mixture to the blueberries; toss to coat the fruit. Fill a pastry-lined deep dish pie plate with the blueberry mixture. Drizzle with the lemon juice and dot with the butter or margarine. Adjust the top crust. Seal and flute the edges. Bake for 45 minutes, or until the crust is golden brown.

MAKES 6 TO 8 SERVINGS

BLUEBERRY PUDDING

New England and the Deep South, where traditions die hard, are the last holdouts of serious pudding appreciation in the United States. It is rare to find a town diner in the Northeast that doesn't have at least a few puddings on its lunch menu: tapioca, rice, bread and butter, Indian. Durgin-Park once offered ten different kinds every day.

2	*cups blueberries*
1½	*teaspoons lemon juice*
½	*teaspoon cinnamon*
¾	*plus 1 cup sugar*
3	*tablespoons butter*
½	*cup milk*
1	*cup flour*
1	*teaspoon baking powder*
¼	*teaspoon salt*
1	*tablespoon cornstarch*
1	*cup boiling water*

Preheat the oven to 375°F. Mix together the berries, lemon juice, and cinnamon and spread the mixture in a well-greased, 8 x 8-inch pan. Cream the ¾ cup sugar with the butter, and add the milk. Sift together the flour, baking powder, and salt, and add to the butter mixture. Spread this batter over the berries. Mix together the remaining 1 cup sugar with the cornstarch plus a dash of salt, and sprinkle this mixture over the batter. Pour the boiling water over the top, but do not stir it in. Bake for 1 hour. Serve with whipped cream or ice cream.

MAKES 4 SERVINGS

BLUEBERRY SOUR CREAM COFFEE CAKE

For breakfast or for snacks any time of day, this simple cake is also suitable as the conclusion to a lobster dinner. Serve it warm.

1½	cups flour
½	cup plus ½ cup sugar
½	cup margarine
1½	teaspoons baking powder
1	egg plus 2 egg yolks
1	plus 1 teaspoon vanilla
1	(1-quart) bag frozen blueberries
2	cups sour cream

Preheat the oven to 350°F. In a mixing bowl combine the flour, ½ cup sugar, margarine, baking powder, 1 egg, and 1 teaspoon vanilla. Mix thoroughly; turn into a greased, 10-inch tube pan. Sprinkle with the berries. In another bowl combine the sour cream, egg yolks, the remaining ½ cup sugar, and the remaining teaspoon vanilla. Blend well. Pour over the berries. Bake for 1 hour.

MAKES 1 CAKE

BROWNIES

Many modern brownies are super-rich, ultra-chocolaty, and so moist they verge on being half-cooked cake batter. That is not necessarily a bad thing, but if you crave a brownie that has a less assertive character, more like cake, this recipe is the one to use.

3	*(2-ounce) squares chocolate*
½	*cup margarine*
3	*eggs*
1½	*cups sugar*
1	*cup flour*
¾	*teaspoon baking powder*
½	*teaspoon salt*
1½	*teaspoons vanilla*
¾	*cup chopped walnuts*

Preheat the oven to 350°F. In a saucepan melt the chocolate and margarine. In a mixing bowl beat the eggs until thick and add the sugar. Beat in the chocolate mixture. Stir in the flour, baking powder, salt, vanilla, and walnuts. Bake in a greased and floured 9 x 9-inch pan for 40 minutes.

MAKES 16 TO 18 BROWNIES

BOSTON CREAM PIE

We cannot tell a lie: Boston Cream Pie is the one dessert on the menu that is *not* actually made in the Durgin-Park kitchen. But so many visitors want to have it as part of their traditional Boston meal that it is always available. Why it's called pie rather than pudding-cake is a mystery food historians have yet to satisfactorily explain.

Cake:

1½	sticks (¾ cup) unsalted butter, softened
1¼	cups sugar
1	teaspoon vanilla
2	large eggs
2	cups cake flour
2½	teaspoons double-acting baking powder
½	teaspoon salt
¾	cup milk

Custard:

3	tablespoons cornstarch
⅓	cup sugar
1	cup milk
3	large eggs
½	cup heavy cream
¼	teaspoon salt
1	vanilla bean, split lengthwise
3	tablespoons unsalted butter

Glaze:

6	*ounces fine-quality bittersweet chocolate*
3	*tablespoons water*
2	*tablespoons unsalted butter*
1½	*tablespoons corn syrup*
¼	*teaspoon salt*

Seasonal fruit, for garnish

To make the cake, preheat the oven to 350°F. Prepare a 9½-inch springform pan. In a medium bowl cream together the butter, sugar, and vanilla until light and fluffy and beat in the 2 eggs, one at a time, beating well after each addition. In a separate bowl sift together the flour, baking powder, and salt and beat into the butter mixture in batches alternately with the milk, beginning and ending with the flour mixture. Pour the batter into the prepared springform pan and bake the cake in the middle of the oven for 50 to 55 minutes or until a tester comes out clean. Let the cake cool in the pan on a rack.

To make the custard, in a saucepan whisk together the cornstarch, sugar, and milk. Add the eggs, cream, and salt and whisk the mixture until it is smooth. Add the seeds from the vanilla bean, reserving the pod, to the cream mixture and bring to a boil over moderate heat, whisking constantly, for 2 minutes. Remove the pan from the heat and whisk in the butter. Let the custard cool completely, whisking occasionally.

To make the glaze, in a double broiler melt the chocolate with the water, butter, corn syrup, and salt, stirring until the glaze is smooth. Take off the heat when melted through. Cut the cake in half horizontally and place the bottom half on a plate. Top the bottom half with the custard, spreading it to the edge. Put the remaining cake half, cut side down, on the custard and pour the glaze on top, spreading it to the edge and letting it drip down the side. Garnish the pie with the fruit.

MAKES 1 CAKE

CARAMEL BREAD PUDDING

Bread pudding is all-American, but each region has its own special way of making a deeply satisfying dessert out of yesterday's stale bread. This is the kind of recipe that nutritionists of the early twentieth century used to recommend as health food, especially for growing children: plenty of butter, milk, and eggs.

1	cup brown sugar
	Butter
5	slices of bread
3	cups milk
⅛	teaspoon salt
2	eggs, beaten
1	teaspoon vanilla

Preheat the oven to 350°F. Place the sugar in the bottom of a buttered casserole or baking dish. Butter the bread, remove the crusts, cut the slices into quarters, and place on top of the sugar. Mix the milk, salt, eggs, and vanilla and pour over the bread. Bake for about 40 minutes, or until a knife inserted in the middle comes out clean. Serve with top milk (half-and-half), cream, or ice cream.

MAKES 5 TO 6 SERVINGS

THE BOSTON TEA PARTY

The Boston Tea Party was political theater at its finest. It came as a climactic protest against British tax policies, which the American colonists were fighting by means of a very effective boycott of imported tea. Up and down the Atlantic seaboard, patriots turned away ships that were carrying the tea, but when the *Dartmouth, Eleanor,* and *Beaver* made it into Boston Harbor in 1773 carrying tea for the East India Company, the Sons of Liberty, led by Samuel Adams, decided something dramatic had to be done.

On December 16 in the evening, three companies of fifty men masquerading as Mohawk Indians and carrying tomahawks and axes boarded the ships. As thousand of spectators looked on, the men broke open the tea chests and tossed 342 crates of Darjeeling into the harbor. About nine o'clock when it was over, the patriots walked from the wharf with a fife playing a triumphant tune. They are said to have marched past the home of British Admiral Montague, who had seen the whole event. Montague called out, "Well boys, you had a fine, pleasant evening for your Indian caper, haven't you? But mind, you have got to pay the fiddler yet!"

Parliament closed the Port of Boston and passed an act that allowed the quartering of troops in colonists' barns and houses. The new "Coercive Acts" led to further protests all along the seaboard. Although the tea party was itself peaceful, it was a significant step on the road to armed revolution.

CINNAMON-APPLE CAKE

A gentle-textured spice cake is suitable for dessert, afternoon or midnight snacks, or breakfast. If serving it for dessert, you might want to accompany each serving by a cup of Hard Sauce (page 178) and a small knife to spread it on the cake.

1½	cups plus ¼ cup sugar
½	cup margarine, softened
1	teaspoon vanilla
6	ounces cream cheese, softened
2	eggs
1½	cups all-purpose flour
1½	teaspoons baking powder
¼	teaspoon salt
2	teaspoons cinnamon
3	cups peeled, chopped Rome apples

Preheat the oven to 350°F. Beat the 1½ cups sugar, margarine, vanilla, and cream cheese at medium speed until well blended, about 4 minutes. Add the eggs one at a time, beating well after each addition. Combine the flour, baking powder, and salt, and fold into the creamed mixture, beating at low speed until blended. Combine the remaining ¼ cup sugar with the cinnamon. Combine 2 tablespoons of the sugar and cinnamon mixture and the apples in a bowl and stir the apple mixture into the batter. Pour the batter into an 8-inch, springform pan coated with cooking spray and sprinkle with the remaining cinnamon mixture. Bake for 1 hour 15 minutes, or until the cake pulls away from the sides of the pan. Cool completely on a wire rack, and cut with a serrated knife.

MAKES 1 CAKE

HERMITS

We don't know for sure, and culinary history doesn't seem to yield any clues, but we have always assumed that hermits got their name because they are a homely, unspectacular dessert. If a food could be said to be shy and retiring, they are. Unlike a big, fudgy brownie or glistening cinnamon roll or broad-topped muffin, they don't call out with a siren song from their pastry pedestal. And yet you see them in diners and bakeries throughout the Northeast; they are an incredibly popular pastry for breakfast, as well as for dessert.

2	*cups raisins, chilled*
½	*cup margarine*
1½	*cups sugar*
2	*eggs*
2	*cups flour*
1	*teaspoon baking soda*
1	*teaspoon salt*
1	*teaspoon cinnamon*
½	*teaspoon ground cloves*
1	*teaspoon nutmeg*
½	*cup walnuts, chopped* (optional)

Cover the raisins with cold water and boil 15 minutes. Drain and cool. Preheat the oven to 350°F. Cream the margarine and sugar until light and fluffy. Add the eggs one at a time, beating well after each addition. In a separate bowl sift the flour, baking soda, salt, cinnamon, cloves, and nutmeg together. Add to the creamed mixture. Add the chilled raisins and nuts. Fold in thoroughly. Bake on a well-greased, jelly roll pan for 30 minutes. Cool in the pan and cut into squares.

MAKES 10 TO 12 SERVINGS

COFFEE JELL-O

Coffee Jell-O is a big surprise—a thanks-I-needed-that slap in the face. What's shocking about it is how unlike ordinary Jell-O it is, hardly sweet at all except for whatever whipped cream you put atop it. It is serious, dark, and stolid, which is why we consider it a Durgin-Park standard-bearer. Like the restaurant itself, it is what it is, and it doesn't try to charm you by its sweetness.

1	quart coffee (leftover is better)
¾	cup sugar
2	envelopes unflavored gelatin

In a saucepan bring the coffee to a boil. Whisk in the sugar and gelatin until dissolved. Place the coffee mixture in a shallow pan and refrigerate for 2 to 4 hours, or until firm.

MAKES 6 SERVINGS

ICE CREAM PIE

The Northeast is the cradle of important ice cream: HoJo's began in Massachusetts, Ben & Jerry's in Vermont, Haagen-Dazs and Carvel in New York State. To this day, New England eats more ice cream per capita than any other region of the country. Usually, it's served in cups or cones, but this recipe is a deluxe variation. Feel free to serve it topped with hot fudge or chocolate sauce.

	Vanilla wafers
1	*cup evaporated milk*
1	*cup tiny marshmallows*
1	*(6-ounce) package chocolate bits*
	Dash of salt
2	*pints vanilla ice cream*
1	*cup walnuts*
	Whipped cream

Line the bottom and sides of a 9-inch pie pan with the vanilla wafers. In a double boiler combine the milk, marshmallows, chocolate bits, and salt. Over medium-low heat cook and stir until thick. Cool the sauce. Spoon 1 pint of the ice cream over the vanilla wafers. Drizzle half the sauce over the ice cream. Spoon on the second pint of ice cream. Drizzle the remaining sauce over the ice cream. Place in the freezer. Remove from the freezer 15 minutes before serving. Top with the walnuts and whipped cream.

MAKES 8 SERVINGS

MAPLE UPSIDE-DOWN CAKE

There is no single flavor that is more distinctly Yankee than maple. While good maple syrup is produced in other parts of the country, it is in the Northeast that cooks have found the most ways to use it as the linchpin of recipes for desserts, breads, roasts, and vegetables. For cooking purposes, grade A light amber (the most refined and most expensive kind) is too delicate-flavored. In this delicious cake, we recommend using grade A dark, which has a powerful maple flavor.

1	*tablespoon butter, at room temperature*
3	*tablespoons sugar*
1	*large egg, beaten*
1	*cup all-purpose flour*
2	*teaspoons baking powder*
½	*teaspoon grated nutmeg*
	Speck of salt
½	*cup milk*
1	*cup maple syrup*
½	*cup chopped walnuts*
	Whipped cream for topping

Preheat the oven to 400°F. Butter an 8-inch round cake pan. In a large saucepan combine the butter and sugar and heat for 7 minutes, until light and fluffy. Remove from the heat and add the egg. Beat for 3 minutes longer, or until the batter is lemon colored. In a medium mixing bowl whisk together the flour, baking powder, nutmeg, and salt. Add the flour mixture to the butter mixture alternately with the milk, beginning and ending with the dry ingredients; blend well.

In a small saucepan bring the maple syrup to a boil. Pour the syrup into the cake pan, sprinkle in the nuts, and then slowly pour the batter over the syrup and nuts, patting it into the pan with a rubber spatula. (If you have trouble with this, don't worry; the cake will bake out to the edges, just as it should.) Bake the cake for 30 minutes or until it is golden brown and the syrup is bubbling up around the edges. Cool in the pan for 10 minutes and then invert onto a plate. Serve warm with whipped cream topping.

MAKES 1 CAKE

MINCEMEAT

Mincemeat is one of those colorful dishes that was invented as a way to prevent spoilage (like chili and curry). The idea was to pot beef with plenty of spice and fruit and ample alcoholic spirits so it was always ready to bake into a pie that was on the cusp of sweet and savory. Most modern store-bought mincemeats are simply fruits and spices without the beef and suet, but this Durgin-Park recipe is the real deal. Use it in full-size pies or small, individual tarts.

2	pounds lean beef, finely chopped
2	pounds suet, finely chopped
3	quarts apples, finely chopped
3	pounds raisins, chopped
2	pounds currants
1	pound citron, finely chopped
½	cup chopped candied orange peel
½	cup chopped candied lemon peel
½	cup lemon juice
¼	cup orange juice
2	tablespoons salt
4	cups sugar
2	cups cider
1	teaspoon ground cloves
1	teaspoon allspice
2	teaspoons ground cinnamon
1	cup currant jelly
3	cups brandy

In a large crock pot mix all the ingredients except the brandy and cook for 2 hours. When cool, add the brandy. Let the mixture stand in the crock pot for a week before using. The mincemeat will keep indefinitely in a cool place.

MAKES 12 QUARTS

MOLASSES COOKIES

The basic molasses cookie has been a favorite sweet since Colonial days, its best-known incarnation known as a *Joe frogger* after a Marblehead, Massachusetts, man who made plump little spice cookies that resembled the frogs in his pond. Local fishermen were said to like his cookies so much that they traded Uncle Joe jugs of rum for the cookies, which they took with them out to sea.

¾	cup shortening
⅓	cup molasses
1	cup sugar plus extra for dipping
1	egg, beaten
2	cups flour
½	teaspoon salt
1	teaspoon cinnamon
½	teaspoon ground ginger
¼	teaspoon cloves
2	teaspoons baking soda

Preheat the oven to 350°F. In a large bowl beat together the shortening, molasses, sugar, and egg. In a separate bowl sift together the flour, salt, cinnamon, ginger, cloves, and baking soda; mix into the molasses mixture. Shape the dough into small balls and dip them in the sugar. Place the dough on an ungreased cookie sheet. Bake for 8 to 10 minutes. Cool on pan.

MAKE 3 TO 4 DOZEN

PLUM PUDDING

It takes a lot of time and some effort to make a real plum pudding, but the result is a holiday dessert that sings of a loving kitchen. This type of pudding, which is steamed for hours, is less like the more familiar kinds of dessert puddings such as rice pudding or tapioca. It is more cakelike . . . and it has a rich character that is beyond description. Serve it topped with Hard Sauce (page 178).

8	ounces candied fruit, chopped	¼	teaspoon salt
¼	pound suet	1	cup light brown sugar
½	cup blanched almonds	1	cup bread crumbs
½	cup chopped walnuts	½	cup flour
1	cup chopped apple	3	eggs
1	cup raisins	¼	cup dark molasses
1	cup currants	½	cup milk
½	teaspoon cinnamon		Boiling water
½	teaspoon nutmeg	⅔	cup brandy
½	teaspoon cloves		
½	teaspoon ginger		

In a large bowl combine the candied fruit, suet, almonds, walnuts, apple, raisins, currants, spices, salt, brown sugar, bread crumbs, and flour. In a separate bowl beat the eggs until thick and add the molasses and milk. Add to the fruit mixture; stir well. Pour into a well-greased mold and cover with greased brown paper. Place in an 8-quart pan and fill with boiling water to cover half way up the side of the mold. Cover the pot. Steam for 4 hours. Serve warm with Hard Sauce and whipped cream.

MAKES 10 TO 12 SERVINGS

HARD SAUCE

There are few desserts that hard sauce does not complement well. After all, it is nothing but sugar and butter with a dash of brandy for flavoring. We especially like it as an alternative to ice cream for topping warm Indian pudding.

5	*tablespoons butter*
1	*cup confectioners' sugar*
2	*tablespoons brandy*

In a bowl cream the butter then slowly add the sugar, beating well until creamy. Add the brandy and blanch. Cover and refrigerate.

MAKES 1 CUP

PIE CRUST

At Durgin-Park a nine-inch pie serves no more than six people, but if you plan on cutting normal-sized portions, this pie crust will enclose enough for at least eight.

2¾	*cups flour*
	Pinch of salt
1	*cup solid vegetable shortening*
1	*egg*
1	*teaspoon distilled white vinegar*
⅓	*cup ice water*

Sift the flour and salt into a bowl, cut in the shortening, and mix until the dough resembles bread crumbs. In a separate bowl beat the egg, vinegar, and water and pour into the dough all at once. Continue cutting until the flour is damp and forms clumps. Turn the dough into a lightly floured bowl and gently knead until smooth, adding a few more drops of water if necessary. Divide the dough in half and roll to the size of a 9-inch, flat, round cake. Fit into a pie plate. Refrigerate the second half until ready to use.

MAKES TWO 9-INCH CRUSTS

POUND CAKE

Pound cake is customarily served plain with coffee in Yankee homes, but if you have a serious sweet tooth and want to be completely heretical, you can use it instead of a biscuit to make strawberry shortcake.

1	cup butter
1¾	cups superfine sugar
4	eggs
1	teaspoon vanilla
1	teaspoon lemon extract
1	cup milk
3	cups cake flour
½	teaspoon baking powder
½	teaspoon baking soda
¾	teaspoon salt

Preheat the oven to 300°F. In a mixing bowl cream the butter, adding the sugar gradually. Add the eggs one at a time, beating well after each addition. Add the vanilla and lemon extract. In a separate bowl sift the dry ingredients together and add them to the egg mixture alternately with the milk, beginning and ending with flour. Pour the mixture into a greased and floured tube pan. Bake for 1 hour 15 minutes. Cool in the pan on a rack for 5 minutes before removing the cake.

MAKES 1 CAKE

PUMPKIN PIE

Pumpkin pie is a de rigueur dessert at supper tables starting at Thanksgiving and continuing through the winter holidays. No matter what *other* pies are served on Turkey Day or at Christmastime—apple is vital, too—it just wouldn't be right to have a festive cold-weather meal without ending it with the spicy, creamy taste this pie delivers.

1	(16-ounce) can pumpkin
1	cup sugar
1	teaspoon ground cinnamon
1	teaspoon ginger
1	teaspoon nutmeg
½	teaspoon salt
1	egg
⅔	cup (5½-ounce can) evaporated milk
1	cup milk
	Pastry for single-crust pie

Preheat the oven to 375°F. In a large mixing bowl combine the pumpkin, sugar, cinnamon, ginger, nutmeg, and salt. Add the egg and with a fork lightly beat it into the pumpkin mixture. Add the milks; mix well. Place the pastry in a deep dish pie plate on an oven rack and pour in the pumpkin mixture. Bake for 45 minutes or until a knife inserted off center comes out clean.

MAKES 6 TO 8 SERVINGS

RAISIN SPICE CAKE

A pastry that travels extraordinarily well, raisin spice cake is well-suited for taking to picnics or potluck suppers. If serving at home, it's nice iced; if carrying it elsewhere, un-iced is fine, too.

1	cup raisins
1	cup chopped nuts
1	cup boiling water
1	teaspoon baking soda
½	cup shortening
1	cup sugar
3	egg yolks and 1 egg white
1	teaspoon cinnamon
1	teaspoon vanilla
1	teaspoon lemon juice
1½	cups flour
¼	teaspoon salt

In a large bowl soak the raisins and nuts in the water and soda; let stand. Preheat the oven to 325°F. In another bowl cream the shortening and sugar until fluffy. Beat the egg yolks and egg white together until thick. Stir in the cinnamon, vanilla, and lemon juice. Mix in the flour, salt, raisins, and nuts alternately. Pour into an 8-inch tube pan, and bake for 1 hour 15 minutes.

MAKES 1 TUBE CAKE

RHUBARB PIE

When rhubarb, known as "pie plant," appears in gardens—and subsequently in pies of home kitchens and restaurants—it's a sure sign of spring in New England. Its felicitous sweet-tart nature seems particularly well-suited to the local insistence on desserts . . . but desserts that are not cloyingly sweet.

3	*eggs*
⅛	*plus ⅛ cup sugar*
¼	*cup margarine or butter*
¼	*teaspoon salt*
¼	*cup all-purpose flour*
2½	*cups chopped rhubarb*
1	*unbaked pie shell*

Preheat the oven to 375°F. Separate the eggs. Beat the egg whites and ⅛ cup sugar until stiff. Mix the egg yolks, margarine or butter, salt, remaining ⅛ cup sugar, and flour thoroughly. Fold in the rhubarb, and then the reserved meringue. Pile into the pie shell. Bake on the bottom rack for 15 minutes. Reduce the heat to 325°F and bake for 30 minutes more. Serve at room temperature.

MAKES 6 TO 8 SERVINGS

RICE PUDDING

You don't need to garland this classic rice pudding with the faint crunch of a burnt-sugar topping, but it gives the dish a shot of excitement that the ordinarily mild-mannered dessert seldom has.

Pudding:

1	cup water
1	cup uncooked, long grain rice
4	cups milk (1 cup low-fat milk)
1	large egg
½	cup sugar
1	teaspoon vanilla
¼	cup orange juice
1½	teaspoons grated orange peel

Brûlé Topping:

3	tablespoons sugar
½	teaspoon cinnamon

Bring the water to boil in a 3-quart saucepan. Stir in the rice and reduce the heat. Cover and simmer for 5 minutes or until the water is absorbed; stir occasionally. Stir in the milk and bring to a boil. Reduce the heat. Cover and simmer for 25 minutes or until the rice is soft; stir occasionally. Whisk the egg, sugar, and vanilla in a medium bowl until blended. Gradually stir in the hot rice. Return to the saucepan and stir for 1 minute over medium-low heat to cook the egg. Remove from the heat and stir in the orange juice and peel. Pour into a 1½-quart, broiler-proof dish and refrigerate for at least 1 hour until the pudding is chilled and set.

To serve, heat the broiler. Combine the sugar and cinnamon and sprinkle evenly over the pudding. Broil four inches from the heating element for 5 minutes or until sugar melts and starts to caramelize. Serve warm or chilled.

MAKES 10 SERVINGS

STEAMED MOLASSES PUDDING

An old England tradition that became part of New England heritage, steamed puddings are a rarity in modern restaurants and home kitchens. It takes some time, effort, and commitment to do one right, but the reward is a lavish "duff" with character beyond ordinary cake or pie.

Pudding:

1	cup all-purpose flour
1	teaspoon baking powder
½	teaspoon salt
½	cup golden, seedless raisins
1	large egg
½	cup light molasses
½	cup milk
½	cup vegetable oil

Orange Sauce:

1	cup sugar
1	tablespoon all-purpose flour
½	cup water
½	cup orange juice
1	tablespoon fresh lemon juice
1	tablespoon butter
½	teaspoon ground cinnamon

Grease and flour a 3-cup pudding mold or ovenproof bowl. Place a rack and water in the bottom of a vegetable steamer—the water should not touch the pudding mold—and bring to a boil. In the meantime, in a large bowl whisk together the flour, baking powder, and salt. Add the raisins and toss together to mix. In a small bowl beat the egg and then add the molasses, milk, and oil; beat until combined. Pour the molasses mixture over the dry ingredients and blend with a mixing spoon; the batter will be very runny. Pour into the prepared mold, cover with its lid or foil, place it on the steamer rack, and lower it into the steaming kettle. Cover and steam for 1 hour.

To make the sauce, in a small saucepan whisk together the sugar and flour. Heat the water and orange juice (I do this in a measuring cup in the microwave) and whisk it into the sugar mixture. Cook and stir over medium-high heat until the mixture is thickened, about 2 minutes. Add the lemon juice, butter, and cinnamon and cook for 1 minute longer. Keep warm.

Remove the pudding mold from the steamer and let it stand for 10 minutes. Loosen the edges with a knife and tip out onto a serving plate. Cut into wedges and serve with the hot orange sauce.

[Note: This dessert reheats very well in the microwave.]

MAKES 8 SERVINGS

STRAWBERRY SHORTCAKE

If you have eaten strawberry shortcake only in the Midwest, South, or West, it is likely this recipe will seem strange to you. For unlike most of the rest of the country, New Englanders like their strawberry shortcake made not out of cake, but out of biscuits. In fact, that's what this recipe yields: two giant biscuits that should be buttered warm from the oven, then quickly layered with fresh, sweetened strawberries and whipped cream—real, freshly whipped cream, please!

2	cups flour
3	teaspoons baking powder
1	teaspoon salt
2	teaspoons plus 1 cup sugar
½	cup shortening
¾	cup milk (approx.)
2	quarts large, ripe strawberries
	Whipped cream

Preheat the oven to 450°F. Mix and sift together the flour, baking powder, salt, and the 2 teaspoons sugar. Cut in the shortening until well mixed. Add the milk, stirring quickly to make a soft dough. Turn onto a lightly floured board and pat with your hands just enough to shape. Cut into two cakes, each ½-inch thick. Bake for 15 minutes. Slice the strawberries into a bowl. Add the remaining 1 cup sugar. When the cakes are done, remove them from the oven and butter each layer. Spread the berries on each buttered layer, topping the second layer with the whipped cream.

MAKES 6 SERVINGS

STRAWBERRY PIE

Strawberry pie is one of Durgin-Park's signature desserts and is always available, even in cold-weather months, almost always made from fresh strawberries. When fresh ones are not available, this pie is a good alternative, as the freshness of the berries is immaterial to its flavor.

¾	*cup sugar plus sugar to sweeten topping*
2	*egg whites*
1	*teaspoon lemon juice*
⅛	*teaspoon salt*
½	*plus ½ cup whipped cream, unsweetened*
2	*(10-ounce) packages frozen strawberries*
1	*(9-inch) baked pie crust*

In a bowl beat the sugar, egg whites, lemon juice, and salt. Fold ½ cup whipped cream into the egg whites. Fold in the strawberries. Put in the pie crust. Refrigerate or freeze. Sweeten the remaining whipped cream; use for a topping.

MAKES 6 TO 8 SERVINGS

TOLL HOUSE COOKIES

Chocolate chip cookies are one of New England's best-appreciated contributions to the American diet. They were originally made at Kenneth and Ruth Wakefield's Toll House, a long-gone restaurant in Wakefield, Massachusetts (near Boston), of which traveling trencherman Duncan Hines sang these praises in his book, *Adventures in Good Eating*: "Its furnishings, fresh flower arrangements, excellent food, and pleasing service, combined with its delightful host and hostess, make it one of my outstanding favorites." Of the many things Hines liked to eat, the cookies Mrs. Wakefield made have endured as part of this nation's confectionery culture.

1	cup margarine
12	tablespoons sugar
12	tablespoons light brown sugar
1	teaspoon vanilla
2	eggs
2¼	cups flour
1	teaspoon baking soda
¾	teaspoon salt
1	tablespoon water
1	(1-pound) bag chocolate bits
	Walnuts (optional)

Preheat the oven to 375°F. Cream the margarine and sugars; add the vanilla and eggs. In a separate bowl sift the flour, soda, and salt together. Add the water to the sugar and egg mixture and stir in the dry ingredients. Fold in the chocolate bits and walnuts. Bake on a greased cookie sheet for 8 to 10 minutes.

MAKES 2½ DOZEN

• DRINKS •

LEMONADE

Before everybody had a refrigerator (once known as an icebox), ice was a luxury item, a fact that might explain why parsimonious cooks of the Northeast tend to serve cold beverages with only a few ice cubes. Or maybe the dearth of ice in cold beverages is simply a sensible way to keep them from being diluted by the water.

12	*lemons*
1¼	*cups sugar*
3	*quarts spring water*

Lemons should be at room temperature. Roll to soften, and then squeeze, cut, and remove the seeds, but not the fruit pieces. In a bowl mix the lemon juice, sugar and water together. Stir well to dissolve. Taste and add more sugar if needed. Chill well.

MAKES ABOUT 3½ QUARTS

MULLED CIDER

It is especially worth mulling cider in the autumn, when it is fresh-pressed from apples with full flavor. Serve it with plain cake donuts as a cold-weather snack.

½	teaspoon allspice
1	(2-inch) stick cinnamon
6	whole cloves
1	quart cider
½	cup brown sugar
	Grated nutmeg, for garnish

Tie the allspice, cinnamon, and cloves in a cheesecloth bag. Heat the cider in a kettle, and drop in the bag. Add the sugar and let the mixture simmer until the cider is spicy enough. Serve in mugs with a dash of the nutmeg.

MAKES 4 TO 6 SERVINGS

B-52

You don't have to offer the toast of "bombs away!" when you hoist this precisely layered libation, but once it's down the hatch, you will understand why it is named after the heavy, long-range Stratofortress.

½   ounce Kahlúa

½   ounce Bailey's Irish Cream

½   ounce Grand Marnier

In a cordial glass layer the Kahlúa, Bailey's, and Grand Marnier. (In order to layer the drink correctly, pour each layer slowly over the back of a spoon. With a little practice your B-52 will be perfect every time.

MAKES 1 SERVING

DURGIN·PARK BLOODY MARY MIX

When its primary function was as a mess hall for men who worked in or around the market, Durgin-Park was closed on Sundays. Now that it's a favorite among not only tradition-minded Bostonians but also visitors who want a real taste of Beantown, it is open every Sunday at 11:30 in the morning—an ideal time for tackling a tall glass full of Bloody Mary mix, with or without vodka.

1	(46-ounce) can tomato juice (your choice of brand)
1	tablespoon horseradish
	Several drops of pepper sauce
1	teaspoon steak sauce
2	ounces Worcestershire sauce
1	teaspoon pepper
½	teaspoon salt
½	teaspoon mustard
3	ounces lime or lemon juice

In a pitcher or half-gallon container, pour the tomato juice. Stir in the horseradish, pepper sauce, steak sauce, Worcestershire sauce, pepper, salt, mustard, and lime juice. Chill, or serve over ice.

MAKES 5 TO 6 SERVINGS

DURGIN-PARK BLOODY MARY

While no one has accused the Durgin-Park staff of dawdling service, its casual, communal tables do invite the enjoyment of a prolonged lunch among friends and family, suitably initiated by rounds of house-made Bloody Marys.

3½	*ounces vodka*
	Durgin-Park Bloody Mary Mix (page 194)
1	*celery rib*
1	*lime slice*

Fill a 16-ounce glass with ice. Add the vodka and fill to the top with the Durgin-Park Bloody Mary Mix. Garnish with the celery stick and lime slice.

MAKES 1 SERVING

CHIP'S CHOCOLATE MARTINI

We suspect that back when a group of 150 determined colonists dressed in Mohawk garb threw the East India Tea Company's tea off cargo ships into Boston Harbor, not a lot of those brave patriots were aficionados of the chocolate martini! Times have changed . . . and so have people's preferences in adult libations.

3	*ounces vanilla vodka*
½	*ounce white crème de cacao*

Prepare a martini glass by filling it with ice and soda water (or regular water). Pour the vodka and creme de cacao into a shaker and shake for 5 seconds. Empty the martini glass and pour in the vodka mixture. Drizzle the glass with chocolate syrup.

MAKES 1 SERVING

HOT BUTTERED RUM

Practically guaranteed to cure whatever ails you, whether it be physical or emotional, buttered rum is an ideal cozy-time beverage for cold autumn nights by a crackling fireplace.

1	*teaspoon powdered sugar*
½	*cup New England rum*
1	*tablespoon butter*
	Boiling water

Dissolve the powdered sugar in a little boiling water in a heated medium-sized tumbler. Add the New England rum and butter. Fill the glass with boiling water. Stir well and sprinkle grated nutmeg on top.

MAKES 1 SERVING

MARTY'S OLD-FASHIONED EGGNOG

The most old-fashioned thing about this eggnog, other than its unbelievably rich flavor, is the fact that it calls for raw eggs. Today's well-meaning food police warn us that raw eggs can carry salmonella and should never be incorporated into a recipe. Therefore, consider this a historical artifact.

12	eggs, separated
2	quarts cognac
1	pint New England rum
1½	pounds sugar
2	gallons milk

Beat separately the egg whites and yolks. Mix the yolks in a punch bowl with the cognac, New England rum, and sugar. Slowly add the milk. Stir constantly to prevent curdling. Place the beaten egg whites on top. Sprinkle with grated nutmeg. Place in a tub of ice 2 hours before serving.

MAKES APPROXIMATELY 3 GALLONS

NEW ENGLAND BAKED APPLE TODDY

Is it a drink or is it a dessert? It doesn't really matter because a baked apple toddy satisfies the craving for both a soul-warming beverage and a sweet conclusion to a meal. It is possible to make a nonalcoholic toddy by using unfermented apple cider, but for many people the fun of a toddy is how tipsy you get without thinking that you are having anything serious to drink.

1	teaspoon sugar
2	ounces boiling water
½	cup applejack
½	baked apple
	Grated nutmeg, for garnish

Dissolve the sugar in the boiling water. Pour into a medium-sized tumbler and add the applejack and baked apple. Fill the glass two-thirds full of boiling water. After stirring well, sprinkle with grated nutmeg. Serve with a spoon.

MAKES 1 SERVING

INDEX